GW01402631

A Church Shaped for Mission

Study material for groups based on
An Anglican–Methodist Covenant

Compiled by John Cole

Methodist Publishing House

CHURCH HOUSE PUBLISHING

Church House Publishing,
Church House,
Great Smith Street,
London SW1P 3NZ

Methodist Publishing House,
4 John Wesley Road,
Werrington,
Peterborough PE4 6ZP

ISBN 0 7151 5766 3

Published 2002 by Church
House Publishing and the Methodist
Publishing House

Second impression 2003

Copyright © The Archbishops' Council
and the Trustees for Methodist
Church Purposes 2002

All rights reserved. Churches and
Church organizations have permission
to photocopy the four templates (pp.
36–9) for local use only provided the
copies include the above copyright
notice and no charge is made for
them. Any other reproduction, storage
or transmission of material from this
publication by any means or in any
form, electronic or mechanical,
including photocopying, recording, or
any information storage and retrieval
system, requires written permission
which should be sought from the
Copyright and Contracts Administrator,
Church House Publishing, Church
House, Great Smith Street, London
SWIP 3NZ.

Tel: 020 7898 1557
Fax: 020 7898 1449
copyright@c-of-e.org.uk

Typeset in Humanist 9 pt
Printed by Halstan and Co.,
Amersham, Bucks

Contents

Introduction   v

A start-up guide   vi

Six sessions and an optional workshop

Session one: **Perceptions**   1
It's all done by mirrors!
A gentle reminder that what we see of ourselves
and others will always be less than what God sees

Session two: **History**   5
Retelling our stories
Looking at our inheritance in a new light

Session three: **Mission**   9
What is God doing?
Understanding how God's mission shapes Christ's Church
– and how it allows a variety of authentic responses

Session four: **An ordered faith**   13
In search of full visible unity (A)
Do we agree about what we believe?

Session five: **Oversight**   17
In search of full visible unity (B)
What are appropriate forms of oversight?

Session six: **Covenant**   21
God's bow in the clouds
Seven affirmations and six commitments
– a 'covenant' relationship

An optional workshop: **Finding our local priorities**   25
Activities to involve more than the members of a house group

Worship: **A faithful response**   29

Resources   34

Templates   The Inherited Church – The Emerging Church (see p. 7)   36
Belief – Experience (see p. 16)   37
Koinonia (see p. 27)   38
Comparison of the churches (see p. 28)   39

Acknowledgements   40

Introduction

The Common Statement of the Formal Conversations between the Methodist Church of Great Britain and the Church of England was published in December 2001. Like most official reports it is a well-tempered digest of what apparently had been a very lively and creative exchange between the representatives of the two traditions.

We encourage you to read the full text which is published jointly by Methodist Publishing House and Church House Publishing (ISBN 1 85852 218 8, £4.25).

The Common Statement offers a clear 'next step' for the Church of England and the Methodist Church in Great Britain on their journey into full visible unity – an Anglican–Methodist Covenant. It argues for a new way of thinking about ourselves and our place within God's purposes. *We are challenged to let God's mission shape Christ's Church.*

For most local church people the question will be:
- How will these discussions affect us?
- How do they affect what we think about each other?
- How might they change the way we relate to one another?
- How might they increase what we are able to do together locally?

This study guide sets out to translate the key ideas from the Common Statement so that Christ's disciples locally – from any denomination – can begin to explore the implications.

Although individuals on their own can study this book, it is structured in a way that will allow small groups to study the material over six sessions with an optional concluding workshop. Significant quotations from the Common Statement provide the context for a range of activities, questions for discussion and suggestions for Bible study and prayer.

To get the most from this book, some of the activities need to involve the whole congregation in each participating church. Please read the **Start-up guide** carefully to ensure that the preparatory work is in hand before the group meetings begin.

A start-up guide

Please read this section carefully before beginning any group work.

In this study guide:

- Four pages of material are provided for each group session.

- Resources include quotations from the Common Statement, relevant Bible passages and short reflections on the issues raised.

- The material for each group session concludes with a **Programme for group work**.

- Group leaders will need to adjust this to reflect the character of their group.

- All participants are encouraged to read through the material for each session before coming to the group meeting.

- Each group should also have at least one copy of the Common Statement.

- Some method of making and displaying notes will be useful at most sessions.

- It is important that groups should include members of both Anglican and Methodist congregations.

- Christians from other traditions are uniquely well placed to see what is going on between the two traditions and should be encouraged to take a full part.

- Throughout the workshops, if group members want to start making judgements, remember that the question is not 'Do I like this?' or 'Do I not like it?' but 'Is this of God?'

Session one: Perceptions

This first session allows group members to get to know one another – or to deepen the acquaintance that they already have. It is a chance to learn more about ourselves as well as each other.

Participants should be asked to bring a photo of themselves. The group convener needs to provide a hand mirror for use during the session.

Session two: History

This session is about recognizing that the history of our two churches is ongoing – and that the present is where past touches future. How do we carry our two identities through a time of transition and find confidence in a new shared identity?

Paper and pens will be needed.

Session three: Mission

This session is an opportunity to begin looking together at the mission with which churches in the locality are called to engage, and the resources available to those churches if they can learn to cherish each other.

If a decision has been taken to hold a workshop (see below and pp. 25–8), the whole congregation in all participating churches needs to be involved at an early stage in at least two activities: the time chart and the local map.

Session three will in any case involve some preliminary work using a detailed local map. The convener of the group needs to make sure that one is available in as large a format as possible so that everyone can gather round it.

Session four: An ordered faith

This session is about building confidence in our ability to put our common faith into words and 'be answerable for the hope that is in us'.

Paper and pens will be needed.

Session five: Oversight

This session addresses the stereotypes that people have about leadership in each other's churches and explores what needs to be done if Anglicans and Methodists – locally or nationally – are to achieve a pattern of joint decision-making.

The convener needs to find out how the different denominations are organized locally and how responsibility is exercised for the life and mission of the church.

Session six: Covenant

In this final session participants are invited to check where they stand in relation to the 'Affirmations' and 'Commitments' included in the proposed national Covenant.

The session also provides a first opportunity to explore how a covenant might be appropriate in their local situation.

The workshop – Finding our local priorities

A programme, with notes and resources, is provided on pp. 25–8.

A decision to hold a workshop needs to be taken early – with the full involvement of the Methodist Church Council and the Anglican PCC. The right person then needs to be recruited to facilitate the event.

Consultation, planning and 'enthusing' of local congregations will then be needed outside the group if the event is to fire people's imagination. The programme will almost certainly have to be adjusted.

Two months or more may be needed after the group sessions to lead up to the workshop.

A clear programme for following up the workshop is equally important.

Prayer and worship

Suggestions for prayer, worship, and follow-up action are provided for each session in a special Worship section on pp. 29–33.

Also included are ideas on how to feed back the experiences of the group to the local congregations – an important task whether or not you plan to have the workshop.

Resources

The final section in this study guide provides resources for background reading, and useful contacts for follow-up. It concludes with a request for feedback to the denominations nationally.

Templates

These are expanded versions of four outlines found in Session two (pp. 7, 16, 27 and 28) and may be photocopied.

Now that you have prayed about the proposals for a Covenant, and worked through this study guide, how do you answer the question: 'Is this of God?'

Quotation
from the introduction to the Common Statement

Throughout this study guide the paragraph reference number from the full Statement is placed in brackets before each quotation.

(2) Space does not allow a detailed rehearsal of all the study and discussion that the Formal Conversations have undertaken . . .
it is clear that there is sufficient agreement for the two churches to take the next step that was envisaged when the Formal Conversations were set up.

The Conversations believe that they have fulfilled the task that was entrusted to them and hope their work will pave the way for the next stage of unity between Methodists and Anglicans in England.

It's all done by mirrors!

A gentle reminder that what we see of ourselves and others will always be less than what God sees

Knowing ourselves – and where we 'belong'

Ever since the time of John and Charles Wesley, there has been something ambiguous about the relationship between the Methodist Church and the Church of England.

The Wesleys founded an organization, which became a separate denomination. But they themselves remained priests in the Church of England until they died.

Those of us who have grown up in one or other of the two churches will have different memories, different perspectives, on what all this has meant over the years.

Individuals who have transferred from one denomination to the other will have a different story to tell. So will those who still have to be persuaded that sorting out the differences between denominations actually matters! 'I'm a Christian!' they say.

This first session offers us a way of getting into the ideas, the arguments and the proposals contained in the Common Statement of the recent Anglican–Methodist formal conversations. And since the Statement itself starts by looking at memories, perceptions and realities, so should we!

Just what do we know – or think we know – about each other and about ourselves?

Insights from the Bible

1 Corinthians 1.10-17
Note:
■ The self-righteous ones who say 'I follow Christ'
■ Paul's assertion: 'Christ did not send me to baptize'
■ The refusal to use 'the language of human wisdom'

Proverbs 26.23–27.2
Note:
■ Also try: Proverbs 27.19!
■ Archbishop George Carey at the 2001 Forum of Churches Together in England begged for 'a humble realism'

Matthew 5.23-24
followed by

Romans 12
Note:
■ Read the whole of chapter 12 – it is the classic passage familiar from endless services in the Week of Prayer for Christian Unity!
■ But have we really understood what Paul is saying?

Finally:

Romans 14
Note:
■ The reasons for the differences of opinion are no longer relevant
■ What matters is how Paul encourages Christ's disciples to deal with the arguments
■ 'Why do you despise other believers? All of us will stand before God to be judged by him.' (v. 10)

Needed for this session:
● A hand mirror
● Individuals should be asked to bring a photograph of themselves

Stepping out on a journey together

Quotations
from the Common Statement

(Numbers in brackets – see p. vii)

(4) More than anything else it is the simple fact of separate development which means that the two churches find certain things strange about each other.

(5) Both churches have also tended to tell their own story in terms of myths about each other.

Half-truths identified in the Common Statement

- a 'moribund' Church of England in the 18th century;
- Methodism (as part of the Evangelical Revival) bringing the gospel to a population otherwise deprived;
- a Church of England repudiating its protestant character as a result of the Oxford Movement.

The relationship between the two churches was complex and evolving:

(7) Legislation against clergy holding livings in plurality and against non-residence in the parish . . . meant that the clergy, particularly in villages, were more likely to see nonconformists as rivals rather than potential allies; and that feeling was returned, even though many people still identified themselves as 'church *and* chapel'.

By the end of the 19th century, Anglicans and Methodists seemed to be inhabiting different worlds.

Mutual estrangement . . .

(41) The genesis of our division lay more in pragmatic responses to circumstances than in doctrinal disagreements.

(42) Anglican–Methodist separation may be seen as mutual estrangement which has changed both of us so that we cannot now think in terms of returning to where we were. Our culture as well as our theology and practice have developed independently and we will both need to move on if we are to find a new and common future. In this seeking of a new future, we need to bring our whole selves, past as well as present.

If we wish to make the journey set out in this book, there is only one place to start. We must start with ourselves

- as individuals;
- as people with our own place in the local community;
- as people with a variety of personal relationships;
- as participants in the life of a local Christian congregation;
- as members of 'the Body of Christ';
- as part of the whole human race.

We know ourselves, we find our identity, in three key ways:

1. Our memories   2. Our self-image
3. Our perceptions of others

Our relationships with others depend on the truthfulness of the pictures we have built up in these areas.

- Memories can play tricks.
- How we see ourselves may not be at all how others see us.
- Our perception of others – especially people we don't know very well – can be distorted by 'stereotypes' which prevent us from relating openly to the person in front of us.

In this first session, we are invited to share our memories, our self-image and our perceptions as members of different Christian traditions.

'Mirror, mirror, on the wall . . .'

By looking in a mirror, we think we know what we look like. But do we?

Take a close look at a photograph of yourself and then look at yourself in a mirror. The 'laterally inverted' image in the mirror will often be startlingly different when compared with the photograph.

Yet the face we know so well from the mirror is not the face that others see.

Memories

- What are your memories of relationships between Anglicans and Methodists in your locality?
- Which are good memories? Which are embarrassing or bring to mind past hurts?
- What are your stories if you are one of those who has transferred from one denomination to the other?
- What experiences have formed your impressions of the two denominations, if you are linked to another Christian tradition?
- What do you remember of the failed unity scheme of 1972? Does it still hurt?
- How far have these memories pre-formed your current attitudes to the other church and to these new conversations?

How accurate are these memories?

Self-image

- Why do you belong to the denomination you now belong to?
- What are the good things about that denomination?
- What makes you proud to be a member of the Methodist Church, or an Anglican, or your own tradition if it is neither of these?
- Are there things that your church does well that you wish you could share with other churches?

On the other hand

- What features of your church make you feel ashamed or annoyed?
- What could other churches share with you that would improve things?

How accurate is your self-image?

Perceptions

- In what ways do your memories (and how you see your own church) serve to make you critical of the other church?
- If you are a Methodist, why are you not a member of the Church of England? If you are a member of the Church of England, why are you not a Methodist?
- What features of the other church do you find unattractive or annoying?
- How far are the things that you are proud of in your own church also the things that make you critical of the other church?
- If your tradition is neither Anglican nor Methodist, do you find yourself drawn to one rather than the other and, if so, why?

How accurate are your perceptions?

More quotations
from the Common Statement

Breaking down the stereotypes – healing the memories

(37) Strong feelings . . . could continue to keep the two churches apart. These feelings, however caused, arise not only out of present unease but also out of past conflicts . . . Separated Christians easily slip into stereotyping. The stories, the historical memories become distorted.

(38) Such feelings include disappointment, resentment, insecurity and incomprehension. It is vital that they be acknowledged in order that they may be overcome.

Disappointed hopes over the failure of earlier unity proposals have also left painful memories . . . The healing of memories is a necessary part of the healing of the wounds of division in the body of Christ.

(39) Where our ministers and lay people work closely together, in leadership, local mission and theological conversations, these stereotypes are often broken down.

An agreement between our two churches would formally recognise the excellent relationships between Anglicans and Methodists in many spheres of activity and would itself help to promote the ecumenical healing of memories.

(42) Our aim is not to put the clock back, to gloss over differences, and to construct a monochrome unity. It is to harvest our diversity, to share our treasures and to remedy our shortcomings, so that we may enjoy together what we believe God has already given our churches and still holds in store for us.

Session one
Programme for group work

- An opportunity for personal introductions.
- Time spent individually considering our answers to the questions listed on p. 3.
- A sharing of answers in twos or threes.
- The exercise with a hand mirror and a photograph (see p. 2).
- The whole group hears reports of where there are 'discrepancies' – where one person's memory does not accord with someone else's – where someone's self-image as a member of a particular Christian tradition does not match another person's perceptions.
- The group reviews the biblical material (see p. 1) and the quotations from the Common Statement (on pp. 2 and 3).
- Identify lessons learned – about ourselves and about our relationships within the Body of Christ.
- Conclude by offering it all to God in prayer.

Suggestions for prayer, worship, feedback and follow-up are provided on p. 29.

50 years of Anglican-Methodist conversations

1946 – Archbishop Geoffrey Fisher invites the Free Churches to consider 'taking episcopacy into their system'. Methodists respond positively and talks begin.

1950 – *Church Relations in England* – multilateral report

1963 – Report on proposals for a two-stage approach to forming a united church. (58) The majority view was there were no insuperable doctrinal differences. It was felt that in a united church there was unlikely to be a wider range of theological views than in either of the churches separately.

1972 – Despite strong support from Archbishop Michael Ramsey and approval by the Methodist Conference, the General Synod of the Church of England failed to give the proposals a sufficient majority.

1982 – A covenant for unity between Anglicans, Methodists, United Reformed Church and Moravians was also rejected by the General Synod.

1989 – More positively, the General Synod passed the two ecumenical canons (B 43 andB 44) which are the basis of the Church of England's involvement in current local unity arrangements.

1994 – The Methodist Church asked the Anglicans if it was time to start serious talking again.

1996 – The result was the document *Commitment to Mission and Unity* (65) 'We are aware that our separation damages the credibility of our witness in the world to the reconciling purposes of God.'

Recommendations
a) Formal conversations
b) An agenda for local initiatives – as now illustrated in *Releasing Energy* (see p. 34)

1998 – Formal conversations set up. For mandate see next column.

The mandate for the formal conversations

To produce a Common Statement comprising:
a) A **description** of 'visible unity'.

b) An **indication** within this of what the two churches could agree in faith.

c) An **exploration** of outstanding issues, especially that of oversight.

d) A **declaration** by which the two churches formally acknowledge each other as belonging to the one, holy, catholic and apostolic church of Christ, together with the reality and authenticity of their ministries of word, sacrament and pastoral oversight.

e) A formal **commitment** to work together as a result of this new relationship both generally in the life and mission of God's Church and specifically in order to overcome any remaining obstacles to the full visible unity of the two churches.

Retelling our stories

Looking at our inheritance in a new light

Can we draw on a common memory of our divided history as we rebuild Christ's Church for the future?

Meeting again – after 200 years!

Newspapers sometimes carry stories of brothers or sisters, separated at childhood who rediscover each other in later life. It is an emotional reunion – with many mixed feelings. They know they want to be close, but they know they have a great deal to tell each other. They have their whole life stories to share.

The Church of England and the Methodist Church as we know them today are just like these estranged relatives. We have our own stories to share.

We have been shaped over the years by three overlapping histories – our own denominational histories, and the history of the ecumenical movement during the greater part of the twentieth century. These are the stories of our separation and the record of the mixed fortunes which have marred our attempts to grow together over recent decades.

The stories teach us that both churches are constantly changing and developing – in a constantly changing context.

Any picture that we have of ourselves or of the other tradition can only capture a glimpse of the truth as it was at a particular moment. By the time we have registered it, life has moved on for both of us.

This second session invites us to come to terms with how we feel about changing times – our past, our present, and the future to which God calls us.

Insights from the Bible

The telling of history is always a matter of interpretation.

A: Changing the rules

In the reign of King Josiah they found a book in the Temple. Was it Deuteronomy – the so-called 'Second Law'? (2 Kings 22.8-11) It seems likely:
- 2 Kings 23.1-3 echoes Deuteronomy 10.12-13
- 2 Kings 23.27 echoes Deuteronomy 12.11
- 2 Kings 23.21 echoes Deuteronomy 16

Alternative rules about Passover appear in Exodus 12. How far has history been retold or reinterpreted to validate the changes?

B: A shift of perspective

The Holy Spirit leads us into all truth (John 16.7-15) which is explained as a perspective shift in John 16.21-24: the changed perspective of the mother-to-be once her child has been born.

C: Not clinging to the past

Matthew 10.37-39: taking up the cross means letting go of everything else. 'Those who try to gain their own life will lose it.'

D: A call to transition

Luke 2.8-10: See the Programme for group work (p.8).

E: God's faithfulness

History shows that, in spite of everything
- God fulfils his purposes (Psalm 136)
- God's promises can be trusted (Jeremiah 32)
- and throughout there have been those who were faithful (Hebrews 11)

God's saving purposes are what give history meaning.

The Methodist story
as told in the Common Statement

John Wesley (1703–91)
- Son of the Vicar of Epworth (Lincolnshire), grandson of a distinguished dissenting minister. Upbringing influenced by high-church spirituality and by William Law's *A Serious Call to a Devout and Holy Life*.
- Formed 'The Holy Club' at Oxford with brother Charles – after the style of contemporary 'religious societies'.
- The Wesleys first attracted the name 'Methodist' in 1732 – apparently because of their rigorous rule of life.
- Contact with Moravians and European Pietism while in America (1735–38).

Key dates
1738 – John's conversion experience and switch to open-air preaching.

1744 – First Conference of preachers. The annual 'Conference' has been the central focus of Methodism in Great Britain ever since.

1763 – John's *Notes on the New Testament* and four volumes of sermons included in the model trust deed for Methodist buildings. Thirty-five sermons form a core part of what defines Methodism today.

1784 – John ordains Thomas Coke to be Superintendent for oversight of Methodists in America.

1784 – The 'Legal Hundred' set up to exercise oversight over the movement in perpetuity.

(12) Although Wesley remained a presbyter of the Church of England until his death, it became increasingly difficult to maintain that John Wesley's Methodism was part of the Church of England.

(13) The tensions which Wesley had kept in check during his lifetime exploded after 1791.

An almost continuous story is then told of divisions and reunification, culminating in today's Methodist Church of Great Britain which serves England, Scotland and Wales. This was formed in 1932, bringing together the United Methodists, the Primitive Methodists and the Wesleyan Methodists.

Today
A single 'Connexion' of around 600 circuits in 33 districts – with 2,000 presbyters, 100+ deacons, nearly 10,000 local preachers and a recorded membership of just under 300,000.

A hopeful report

Nearly one quarter of the Common Statement from the formal Anglican–Methodist conversations is spent retelling the histories of the two traditions and of the ecumenical movement.

It suggests that many of the impressions and stereotypes that each tradition has formed of the other have been misplaced. It offers an essentially hopeful account of progress within the ecumenical movement over the last hundred years.

Is this how you see it?

An 'added ingredient' that we will want to take into account is the condition of the two churches today, the opportunities open to them or the problems facing them.

It seems that our churches today confront challenges which are forcing the pace of change and demanding that we re-tell our histories in ways that take us beyond past differences.

Clearly both Anglicans and Methodists in Great Britain, alongside other Christian traditions, are facing unprecedented times. We need all the resources God has given us across all our traditions if we are to keep faith with God's mission and express God's healing love in this generation.

So we cannot think about our histories without also taking stock of our contemporary church life. Past, present and future are completely intertwined.

Some 'here and now' questions – where past touches the future:

- In what ways do you see God challenging and calling you in your particular tradition to find new ways of being 'church' so that people in your wider community can come to experience the good news of Jesus Christ?
- Alternatively, to what extent do you see churches locally and denominations nationally resisting change and putting their efforts into maintaining the status quo?
- How do you balance loyalty to your tradition against the need to find fresh ways of communicating the Gospel in a world which seems to be rejecting old institutional certainties?

Things Anglicans and Methodists already share

- Founder members of the main ecumenical bodies – nationally and worldwide.
- More than half of all Local Ecumenical Partnerships (500+ out of 861) involve both Anglicans and Methodists. 198 of these are two-way partnerships. Many are single congregations sharing worship, mission and pastoral care.
- Huge possibilities exist, locally and between deaneries and circuits – see *Releasing Energy* (details on p. 34).
- Collaboration between national leaders, as well as between bishops and those chairing the Methodist districts.
- Collaboration between central staff teams in areas such as public affairs, education (including joint church schools), care of church buildings etc.

More fundamentally:
Anglicans and Methodists share a common heritage prior to the eighteenth century. Even here, however, we bring the baggage of our own interpretations of the past – and perhaps still need to retell it as a common history.

'Inherited' or 'emerging'?

Statistics suggest that churchgoing in England has been in continuous and often quite steep decline throughout the twentieth century. From this perspective, church unity could be seen simply as a forlorn attempt to 'huddle together to keep warm' during hard times.

More radically, many of those reflecting on the mission of the Church today prefer to speak of a shift from 'inherited' Church to 'emerging' Church.

The old order – when society took its Christianity for granted – has gone. We can no longer simply care for people and assume that sooner or later they'll find their way back to church – a church which is waiting for them unchanged since their childhood.

If people are going to respond to God, we can no longer afford to be preoccupied by the church life that we have inherited from the past. What matters is how we behave as Christ's disciples in the world. In that context, new ways of being 'church' are already emerging.

A template for the group work in Session two

(See p. 36 for expanded photocopiable version.)
Divide a sheet of paper into four and use each quadrant to write your responses to the questions shown below. The exercise can be done by individuals or by keeping a record of group discussion. It will be important to listen to the angels!

The Inherited Church

Angels?
Naming why we feel we can't go on as we are

Demons?
Naming the good things we fear to put at risk

The Emerging Church

Angels?
Naming our calling to be committed to the needs of people around us

Demons?
Naming our fears for the future and the constraints from the present

Meanwhile in the Church of England . . .

The Common Statement identifies two fundamental changes inside the Church of England over the last 150 years:

1. The Oxford Movement of the 1840s

(18) In the 1840s the fear of 'popery' in the Church of England led even the most conservative Wesleyans to ally with Non-conformists almost for the first time. The Evangelical Alliance was one manifestation of this.

These national developments, set alongside an increasing sense of competition between different churches in the towns and villages of England, made the situation in the mid-19th century significantly different from that in previous centuries.

The Lambeth Conference of 1888 sought to remedy this by adopting, as a basis for 'home reunion' (i.e. in the English-speaking world) the four points agreed on by the American bishops in Chicago in 1886.

More than 110 years later, this famous 'Lambeth Quadrilateral' still provides the structure for a key part of the 2001 Anglican–Methodist Common Statement – see Session four (p. 13) and full text (p. 35).

(17) By the end of the 19th century the views of Anglo-Catholics could no longer be ignored.

2. The development of self-government in the Church of England

(19) The Convocations of Canterbury and York – as a result of high church influence – began meeting regularly again from the 1850s.

(20) The 'Enabling Act' of 1919 set up a Church Assembly able to pass measures which, with parliamentary approval, had the force of law.

(20) For the first time since the Reformation this raised the question of whether the Church of England was a distinct body within the nation, as opposed to the nation in its religious aspect . . . The introduction of synodical government in 1969 . . . accentuated this sense of distinctiveness.

(Numbers in brackets – see p. vii)

Twentieth-century ecumenism

A story of a changing climate

(22) The main ecumenical priority for Methodists in the 1920s was internal reunion.

Between the Church of England and the Free Churches, however, the Lambeth Conference of 1920 brought a significant change in relationships:

(21) It no longer seemed daring to join in common prayers or to exchange pulpits, and this became even more frequent after the Second World War.

(22) As the discussions over the Church of South India in the 1930s revealed, Methodism occupied a middle position between Anglicans and Congregationalists.

(21) In the 1940s and 1950s, more ecumenically minded Anglo-Catholics were able to make common cause with 'Liberal Evangelicals', who shared an interest in liturgical revision . . .

By the 1950s,
(23) Among the Free Churches the rapid growth of the 19th century had given way to a gradual and then increasing decline.

(23) *The Free Churches and the State*, a Free Church Council report of 1953, recognised that the 19th-century arguments about disestablishment needed review.

(21) The conservative evangelical strand in the Church of England – continuously present since before Wesley – found a new voice at a historic conference at Keele in 1967.

(24) The Second Vatican Council committed the Roman Catholic Church to ecumenism . . . Thus the Roman Catholic Church became an observer in the discussions among the churches in England in the 1970s about the possibility of a Covenant for Unity.

(25) Areas of Ecumenical Experiment encouraged by the Nottingham Faith and Order Conference of 1964 have grown into the Local Ecumenical Partnerships (LEPs) of today.

Session two
Programme for group work

- The group should be invited to recall lessons from the first session.
- Time spent in twos discussing the 'here and now' questions on p. 6.
- Review whether a picture is emerging of churches facing a time of 'transition' – God moving us from 'inherited' modes of church to new 'emerging' ways of being 'church'.
- A reflection on the story of the shepherds (Luke 2.8-10):

  The shepherds caught a vision – angels with a message of God doing something

  They took time out from their preoccupations – even putting their flocks at risk

  In response to the angels they 'made a transition'

  They found what God was doing in the most unlikely of places

  And there (as tradition has it) they made their gifts.
- An exercise in 'Naming the Demons' and 'Hearing the Angels' in our present situation (see p. 7).
- Acknowledge prayerfully
  1 The tension in ourselves between a) our hankering after our traditions that seem to keep us apart, and b) our longing that the love of God will be experienced afresh in our world.
  2 The deeper dilemma that so often it is in the important 'good things' (inherited or emerging) that we are the most flawed!
- End by offering to God our commitment to seek his priorities and the coming of his Kingdom.

Suggestions for prayer, worship, feedback and follow-up are provided on pp. 29–30.

Following its initial review of the history, the Common Statement offers this conclusion:

(25) The churches are in a new situation today, even by comparison with the position 20 years ago when the English Covenant discussions broke down. Things unimaginable then have now happened. This creates a new openness to different perceptions of hitherto separate histories; it offers a new opportunity to discover and make visible the unity of the Church.

Do you agree?

Session three: Mission
What is God doing?

*Understanding how God's mission shapes Christ's Church
– and allows a variety of authentic responses*

Getting together – to get on with God's work

How can we put into words our experience of what God is doing in his world through Jesus Christ?

The Anglicans and Methodists taking part in the formal conversations have wrestled with this and have put their findings at the heart of their Common Statement.

The writers of the Common Statement offer three major insights and back them up by studying the Bible:

- God's Holy Spirit is active bringing about something in the life of the Church called *koinonia*.

- Christians are called to be engaged in something which is the mission of God, not just the mission of the Church.

- Central to absolutely everything is the incarnate, crucified, raised and glorified Lord Jesus Christ, Son of God and Saviour.

What comes through is a sense that we will only get to know the urgency of the quest for Christian unity when we experience what it means to be called to take our part in God's mission.

The ecumenical calling is about the whole of God's people being engaged with the whole of God's purposes for the sake of God's kingly rule across the whole of God's world.

The next two pages set out the insights that came from the conversations between the representatives in the Anglican–Methodist talks. Groups are invited to explore the Bible passages provided under each heading.

More quotations

'Mission and Unity belong together'

(75) Anglicans and Methodists share a conviction that unity and mission belong together. This is grounded in the indissoluble connection between mission and unity in Scripture – foundationally in John 17.

The Common Statement cites various recent documents:

1. *Commitment to Mission and Unity*

(76) 'The Gospel message . . . is compromised by our divisions, and consequently our witness to reconciliation is undermined. The Church is called to offer the world through its own life the possibility of the unity and peace which God intends for the whole creation.' (*Commitment to Mission and Unity* paragraph 43)

(77) Local ecumenical initiatives, it goes on, 'which are in the vanguard of witnessing to a reconciled and reconciling life', need the authority and support that would come from a national agreement. (*Commitment to Mission and Unity* paragraph 44)

2. *Sharing in the Apostolic Communion*

(78) 'Unity empowers mission, while mission manifests unity and so reveals the true nature of the Church before the world.' (*Sharing in the Apostolic Communion* paragraph 37)

3. *Called to Love and Praise*

(79) [Mission and unity] are bound to be 'closely related . . . since the Triune God who commissions the Church is One, seeking to reconcile and bring the world itself into a unity in Christ'. (*Called to Love and Praise* paragraph 3.2.1)

(Numbers in brackets – see p. vii)

God's Mission and the Church's part in it
as understood in the Common Statement

(85) Mission is grounded in God: it is always God's mission.

(86) 'The Church's task is to participate in God's mission' (*Called to Love and Praise*, paragraph 3.2.12).

(87) Mission is entrusted to the whole Church, not merely to a part of it . . . mission is the vocation and responsibility of all baptised believers, the *laos*, the redeemed and sanctified 'people of his own' (Titus 2.14; cf. 1 Peter 2.9) without distinction between ordained and lay Christians.

(88) Mission addresses the whole person, that is people in all their social, economic, political and cultural relationships.

(89) Within that reality of human living and dying, loving and striving, suffering and rejoicing, God is already at work. We do not attempt to bring an absent Christ to an abandoned world . . . The mission of God to the world is constant and is not restricted to the Church (cf. John 3.16, 5.17) . . . The Church's witness is to the Christ who is at work in his universal mission and is known in his revealed gospel (Acts 1.8).

(90) Mission is not something added on to the being of the Church but is the expression of its essential nature, the cutting edge of its daily life.

Insights from the Bible

'We're on a mission!' says a supermarket advert. St Paul tells us about God's mission:

'Through the Son, God decided to bring the whole universe back to himself.' (Colossians 1.20)

'All this is done by God, who through Christ changed us from enemies into his friends.' (2 Corinthians 5.18)

St John says much the same:

'God loved the world so much that he gave . . .' (John 3.16)

In the letter to Titus, the language has become more technical:

'For God has revealed his grace for the salvation of the whole human race.' (Titus 2.11)

'[Jesus Christ] gave himself for us, to rescue us from all wickedness.' (Titus 2.14)

The newly baptized are told that as a result of 'God's wonderful acts', they are 'the chosen race, the King's priests, the holy nation' (1 Peter 2.9).

The *koinonia* of the Church within God's mission
as understood in the Common Statement

(81) When two or more churches share more and more in local fellowship and mission and explore together theologically what they hold in common,

[1.] They come to a conviction that the *koinonia* that they discern in the other church reflects the *koinonia* that they know within themselves.

[2.] They thus discover a reality of grace in the Spirit that is greater than either of them and which embraces them both.

[3.] They learn to see the Church of Jesus Christ in each other's churches and so to discern the authenticity (although incompleteness) of the ministries, sacraments and forms of oversight within them.

(83) The Church should never be defined merely in terms of its activities as an institution, but always in terms of the character and purpose that it receives from God through grace.

(90) The *koinonia*, mutual participation in Christ, that Christians share is therefore essentially missiological.

(93) The Church is the redeemed community of the God who is Trinity . . . When the Church is united in the truth of Christ, revealed in Scripture, it draws people into the life of God (John 17.20-26).

Koinonia

(83) stands for a full communion with God (2 Corinthians 13:13), a sharing in the very life of God (1 John 1:3), a partaking of the divine nature (2 Peter 1:4).'

Koinonia *cannot be translated by just one English word. It occurs only 19 times in the New Testament – but each occasion is significant – e.g. in the two following passages:*

'The grace of the Lord Jesus Christ, . . . and the *koinonia* of the Holy Spirit be with you all.' (2 Corinthians 13.13)

'What we have seen and heard we announce to you also, so that you will join with us in the *koinonia* that we have with the Father and with his Son Jesus Christ.' (1 John 1.3)

Another 'special' verse is this:
'They "persisted obstinately" in the teaching of the apostles and the *koinonia*, the breaking of the bread, and the prayers.' (Acts 2.42 – translated literally!)

For the inner heart of how Christians experience the *koinonia* of the Spirit, read Philippians 2.1-11.

Christ through whom God's mission is focused
as understood in the Common Statement

(94) The Church's work in mission and unity, indissolubly connected, should reflect the key themes in the unfolding story of God's saving activity in the world.

In other words, the way Christ's disciples are called to follow – in order to be true to God's mission – is the way Christ himself followed.

(75) Both unity and mission are grounded in the truth of God's word as it is revealed definitively in Jesus Christ (John 17.6-8 and 17f.).

Six stages in God's way of reconciliation:
By this means God and humankind can now be 'at one'.

1 Incarnation
(95) Incarnation . . . implies that the unity of the Church must take visible and specific form. Unity . . . must be embodied. Unity proposals must make sense at the local as well as at the national level.

2 Cross
(96) Before the cross, all are in the wrong, all may be put right with God . . . The discovery of unity is costly and calls for a kind of dying.

3 Resurrection
(97) The power of Christ's risen life is at work within the Church and in the world to overcome the forces of alienation and division.

4 Ascension
(98) The ascended Christ intercedes for the unity of his Church . . . (Hebrews 7.25).

5 Christ's sending of the Spirit
(99) The Spirit of Pentecost brings harmony out of discord, unity out of division . . . The Spirit presides over an abundance of different gifts, different stories and different identities. Diversity is cherished; it is gathered together in unity.

6 The final appearing of Christ's Kingdom
(100) The Church on earth embodies God's Kingdom only in imperfect and fragmentary ways . . . Yet it is called to be a sign, instrument and foretaste of the Reign of God.

The Church's witness . . . is distorted when it is itself divided.

Insights from the Bible

For St John, three things are inseparable: God's mission, Christ's self-giving, and the unity of Christ's disciples

'As the Father sent me, so I send you.' (John 20.21)

'Whoever wants to serve me must follow me.' (John 12.26)

'Love one another. As I have loved you, so you must love one another.' (John 13.34)

'Father! May they be in us, just as you are in me and I am in you. May they be one, so that the world will believe that you sent me.' (John 17.21)

But the vision is not exclusive to St John:

'It is not ourselves that we preach; we preach Jesus Christ as Lord, and ourselves as your servants for Jesus' sake.' (2 Corinthians 4.5) Paul was still trying to heal divisions in the Corinthian church!

'Bringing all creation together, with Christ as head' is God's 'secret purpose' in Ephesians 1.9-10.

'You are all one in union with Christ Jesus.' All the usual distinctions are gone in Galatians 3.28.

And our capacity to share in the whole thing – mission, self-giving and unity – is a gift of the promised Holy Spirit:

'The unity which the Spirit gives . . .' is central (Ephesians 4.3) since there is 'One Lord, one faith, one baptism' (Ephesians 4.5) – but diversity of 'gifts' are still needed (Ephesians 4.11-12).

The character of this unity is revealed in the story of Pentecost in Acts 2.5-12. Communion, community and communication (koinonia) are exactly what the Spirit achieved at Pentecost – reversing what happened at the Tower of Babel (Genesis 11.5-9) – a gathering to replace the scattering.

An exercise based on a three-fold understanding of the nature of *koinonia* as communion, community and communication is provided on p. 27 as part of the programme for the optional workshop.

Two pieces of research which will help build awareness of our call to share in God's mission

Even if you have done similar exercises before, doing it with members of two (or more) churches could well produce surprising results.

1 The local map

On a large scale copy of your local area, preferably one which shows street names:

- Locate the churches, the community amenities, the schools.
- Trace the routes people follow to reach these places (including key amenities that lie outside the area).
- Identify the parts of the area where access is most difficult.
- Who lives there? Imagine being very young or very old there. How could church people be 'gospel' to you in that context?
- Where do your church members live – evenly across the area, or in pockets?

What conclusions can you draw?

In your area you will have begun to find many different communities. The Gospel of God's love will initially mean very different things to each of them. In this exercise have you come across any you have not noticed before, any not normally in touch with local churches? Are different churches in touch with different sections of the local population?

2 The church membership

- Find out what proportion of your church members have lived in the area for a long time, even if not in the same house. The proportion will typically be high in rural areas and country towns. If this is the make-up of your congregation, how will you relate to the newcomers?

- Find out what proportion of your church members do not live in the area. The proportion is typically high in many urban, and some suburban and down-town churches. In which case, how will you relate to the residents?

Perhaps if churches with different proportions in their membership exist in the same area, they should recognize that they each have different but complementary vocations as they share in God's mission.

Session three
Programme for group work

- The group should be invited to recall lessons from the second session.
- Time spent in twos and threes – different sub-groups looking at the biblical material cited in support of one of the three insights from this section of the Common Statement (see pp. 10 and 11). This might involve a time of silent reflection and prayer by individuals.
- Each sub-group to present what they think God may be saying to their local churches through their reflection on this insight.
- Start planning the workshop so that it can involve more people from local churches (see p. 25),
- **Or:**

  Explore what is meant by *koinonia* using the material provided for the workshop on p. 27.
- **Or:**

  1. Begin exploring the context in which our local churches operate. Who lives in our area and where? Using a detailed local map, try the exercises in the left hand column.

  2. Try to identify which groups in the community are not in regular contact with our church communities. What could be done to bridge the divide?
- End by offering to God our search for deeper awareness of our shared involvement in his mission in this place. Pray to be shown ways we can make a practical response.

Suggestions for prayer, worship, feedback and follow-up are provided on p. 30.

'The authenticity of our life as churches'

(a phrase used in the foreword of the Common Statement)

Paragraph 81 (highlighted under *koinonia* on p. 10), with its understanding of 'authenticity', is very significant.

It shows how we can cherish different ways of being 'church' within the one Body of Christ.

Do you agree?

Session four: An ordered faith
In search of full visible unity (A)

Do we agree about what we believe?

Knowing God – knowing truth about God

One of the major shifts during the Decade of Evangelism has been from doctrine to spirituality. Yet, in a society where it is generally assumed that any spirituality is OK provided it is authentic for me, how do we know that a particular spiritual experience is Christian?

Previously when people were brought to the Christian faith, this was seen in terms of what they believed about Jesus as their Lord and Saviour. Through the Decade it became clear that coming into Christian faith was much more about what people experienced of the grace of God revealed in Jesus Christ.

Doctrine may be unfashionable, but it is still necessary, and a major part of the Common Statement from the Anglican-Methodist conversations examines what each denomination claims to believe and how they organize themselves as a result. Only in the light of these things can we see how far away the two churches are from 'full visible unity'.

Remarkably, after more than a century, the four key features of 'full visible unity' identified in the conversations are precisely those identified in the Lambeth Quadrilateral of 1888 (see p. 7; full text on p. 35).

1. A common profession of the one apostolic faith grounded in Holy Scripture and set forth in the historic Creeds.
2. The sharing of one baptism and the celebrating of one Eucharist.
3. A common ministry of word and sacraments.
4. A common ministry of oversight (*episcopé*).

The next three pages explore some of the issues discussed in the conversations under the first three headings. A more detailed look at *episcopé*, and at how new patterns of oversight may have to emerge in both churches, forms the task for Session five.

Throughout this session the question is:
Given what the Church of England and the Methodist Church of Great Britain have to say about the Christian faith (doctrine), and how they exercise their discipline as a result, how close is 'full visible unity' between the two traditions and what steps need to be taken to bring it closer?

Note to Group Leaders
The next two pages distil a large amount of detailed discussion in the Common Statement on a range of issues of doctrine and practice. For most people the conclusions are what matter. Groups would be well advised not to debate these issues unless they have the full text of the Common Statement in front of them. Any issues which are 'to be resolved' will be best left to one side. They won't go away!

Insights from the Bible
Teaching and experience

The problem with the word 'teaching' in translations of the New Testament is that it is used indiscriminately for three different words with distinct overtones:

1. What Jesus does is *didache*, the normal generic word for whatever one does to enable learners (disciples).

2. By the (later) pastoral Epistles (Timothy and Titus) a definable body of 'teaching' has accumulated, for which the word is *didaskalia*.

3. Much more rarely, but at significant moments, a word is used from which we get our words 'catechism' and 'catechesis'.

Luke 1.4: had Theophilus been a catechumen?

Acts 18.25: Apollos had certainly been 'thoroughly grounded' in the Scriptures.

Acts 21.21 and 21.24: in both references the word gets close to meaning 'brainwashing'!

Romans 2.18: a touch of sarcasm as Paul asserts that his Jewish reader has had the law 'drummed into him'.

1 Corinthians 14.19: in effect, 'so that other people can grasp the point and not forget it!'

Galatians 6.6: This remarkable sentence from one of St Paul's earliest letters could just about be translated: 'The catechumen should experience *koinonia* with the one catechizing him.'

Words which later gained a technical meaning are already emerging at the heart of Paul's vocabulary. *Koinonia* is seen to be the context for our learning experience.

'A common profession of the one apostolic faith'
The evidence

(103) Both the Church of England and the Methodist Church ground their belief and teaching on the Holy Scriptures, which they hold to be inspired by God. They share the ecumenical Creeds.

Both churches also have secondary, historic formularies. Both churches affirm the apostolic faith in their official formularies and celebrate it in their liturgies and hymnody.

(109) Both traditions recognise that it is the work of the Holy Spirit to bring the text of Scripture to life and to interpret it in the Church.

(Numbers in brackets – see p. vii)

Both give a place to reason, seen as God's gift to be exercised with humility and in deference to the mind of the Church, in discerning the message of Scripture for changed circumstances.

The place of Christian experience in authenticating our appropriation of the faith is tacitly acknowledged in both traditions. The appeal to experience is a thread which runs through the spirituality of Anglicans as well as Methodists.

Verdict:
(110) A careful comparison of Anglican and Methodist formularies and of more recent doctrinal statements will show that the two churches stand side by side in confessing the fundamental apostolic faith as it has been received in the orthodox Christian tradition . . .

(111) Methodists and Anglicans do not necessarily confess the faith in the same idioms or with the emphases always in the same places. Moreover, there is diversity within each of the two churches as well as between them.

Two areas of 'tension'

1. An issue about freewill, divine grace, 'the elect', etc.

The Common Statement argues:
(114) It is not the views of individuals, however influential, that need to be considered when churches seek to reach theological agreement with each other, but the official positions of the two churches as expressed in their formularies or doctrinal standards.

Verdict:
(117) We do not believe, therefore, that this issue . . . should prevent closer union between our churches, any more than it prevents communion within them.

2. The Wesleys' understanding of Christian 'perfection'

The Common Statement argues:
(119) Methodist preachers are not bound to a particular interpretation.

Verdict:
(120) This issue also should not keep our churches apart.

'The sharing of one baptism and the celebrating of one Eucharist'
The evidence

The Common Statement reviews the evidence and concludes:

Baptism
(125) There is agreement between our churches on the theology and practice of baptism.

Membership
(129) Both regard baptism as fundamental initiation into membership of the universal Church. Denominational membership is less clearly defined in the Church of England than in the Methodist Church.

Confirmation
(128) There is basic agreement on the theology of Confirmation – although there is much diversity in both denominations.

(128) The difference between the two churches is confined to the identity of the minister: presbyter or bishop? The Common Statement recognises that this requires further discussion.

Eucharist
(132) As with baptism, so with the Eucharist; both churches responded positively to *Baptism, Eucharist and Ministry* [the important ecumenical statement produced in 1982].

(134) The richness of meaning in the Eucharist has produced different theological emphases.

These are mostly differences within rather than between our churches.

(135) The Common Statement notes the differences between the denominations in handling the bread and wine of communion, the 'sacred elements' – as well as a major difference regarding eucharistic presidency (see next page).

(138) It does not appear . . . that there are any fundamental differences of understanding between us.

(See also next page)

'A common ministry of word and sacraments'
The evidence

The Common Statement offers a specific definition of 'ministry':

(140) All may be called to minister in one way or another. As their ministry is acknowledged and owned by the community, they are seen to act in the name of Christ and his Church.

The Statement then endorses three ecumenically agreed principles:

1. (142) All ministry is the ministry of Christ himself in his body the Church.

2. (143) Baptism incorporates Christians into the community that is called to witness and to serve.

3. (144) The public ministers of the Church represent Christ to his people . . . Ministers also represent the people of God in the ministry of word and sacrament and in public witness before the world,

helping to articulate their faith;

presiding at their worship;

exercising pastoral oversight that is entrusted to the Church as a body.

The Verdict of the Common Statement

On the diaconate
● (147) There seems to be a need for further theological convergence.

On the presbyterate
● (151) 'In the doctrinal clause of the Deed of Union the Methodist Church rejects the idea of a separate priestly caste, claiming exclusive priestly powers and mediating between the Christian and God. We do not believe that these strictures apply to the Church of England's doctrine of presbyteral ministry.'

● (156) A priest in the Church of England is a person called and ordained to the same ministry of word and sacrament as is exercised by ministers within Methodism.

● (157) We believe that there is a common understanding of the presbyterate and that this provides a sound foundation for the eventual interchangeability of presbyteral ministries.

On the episcopate
● (158) The Church of England is a church ordered in the historic episcopate; the Methodist Church in Great Britain at present is not. In spite of this obvious difference . . . we believe that there is a significant convergence in both theology and practice.

● (159) . . . there is substantial agreement in principle . . . Nevertheless, further work remains to be done.

This leads us nicely into Session five!

Koinonia and the sharing of one baptism and one Eucharist

If the lesson of Galatians 6.6 is that our teaching and learning only make sense in the context of *koinonia*, perhaps the same is true of our experience of God's grace.

Without the *koinonia* of the Holy Spirit we will inevitably tend towards the partisan, the sectarian, the judgemental – and eventually we are bound to get it all wrong!

If 'sacrament' is one of the most focused ways in which we experience God's grace, perhaps it is this need for *koinonia* that makes 'one baptism' and 'one Eucharist' so important.

Two ministry matters to be resolved . . .
1. Women in leadership

(161) All posts and positions within the Methodist Church that are open to men are also open to women . . . This principle is regarded as something that the Methodist Church has received from God and wishes to share with the wider Church. For many Methodists, any failure to recognise and accept the full ministry of women would constitute a serious theological obstacle to full visible unity.

(162) The Church of England is currently engaged in an open process of 'reception' . . .

Women bishops already exist elsewhere within the Anglican Communion. However, 'clergy ordained by women bishops elsewhere are not eligible to officiate as clergy in the Church of England.'

2. Who may preside at the Eucharist?

Methodists:
In case of deprivation, named persons are (163) 'authorised by the Conference, for a year at a time, to preside at the Eucharist'.

Church of England:
Presidency is restricted to presbyters (or bishops). (164) 'The presidency over the community's celebration of the Eucharist belongs to those with overall pastoral oversight of the community, i.e. to those ordained as bishop or priest/presbyter' (House of Bishops' report, *Eucharistic Presidency*)

A template for the individual work in Session four

(See p. 37 for expanded photocopiable version.)

Whatever participants write on this paper is for their eyes only.

In the top two panels I can list what I believe – the words of the Nicene Creed might give me a clue (see p. 33).

In the bottom two panels I can record my experience – incidents in the course of my life which have been important on my journey of faith.

BELIEF

The things I believe very strongly

The things I have difficulty believing

EXPERIENCE

The times when God has seemed very close

The times when God has seemed very remote – and it has been hard to stay faithful

---

Before I share any of this with the other participants in my small group, I am free to cross out (or put brackets round) anything that I feel unable to share with them.

I am only being invited to share the things I feel comfortable about sharing.

Session four
Programme for group work

Church members are often tongue-tied because they feel that only professionals can express doctrine accurately. This session shows that we can still 'be answerable for the hope that is in us' (1 Peter 3.15 – note that the word in the Bible is 'hope', not 'faith'!)

● The group should be invited to recall lessons from the third session.

● Participants use the template (left and on p. 38) to write down whatever they can about their own faith.

● In sub-groups of three or four, each participant shares as much or as little of what they have written on the template with the others in the group. It may be worth setting a time limit of three or four minutes per participant. Others in the group should not intervene except to encourage and draw out the speaker.

● In the full group, reflect on the experience:

1. Were people's statements mainly positive, mainly negative or a balance?

2. What proportion of what people wrote were they willing to share?

3. How difficult was it to share what people chose to share? How did others help?

4. Which sections provided the writer with a greater awareness of God? Was it positive or negative material or a balance of both?

5. Did people find many things in common? Were there any denominational differences?

6. Were there any surprises on people's lists – for themselves or in what others shared?

7. How do people now feel towards each other – closer or more distant?

● To summarize, how would we answer these questions?

1. Have we 'shared a common profession of the one apostolic faith'?

2. What have we learned about knowing God?

3. What have we learned about knowing truth about God?

4. What have we learned about the process of sharing? (Was it an experience of *koinonia*?)

● End by offering to God our common faith (and its weakness!) and our experience of God's grace. 'Lord, I believe; help me where faith falls short!'

Suggestions for prayer, worship, feedback and follow-up are provided on pp. 30–31.

So how close are we to 'full visible unity'?

In its final section, the Common Statement takes the discussion about ministry and episcopal oversight a stage further.

See Session five

Session five: Oversight
In search of full visible unity (B)

What are appropriate forms of oversight?

'What Christians hold in common is infinitely greater and more important than what divides them.'

Yes, it's true! And we have seen conclusive proof in the Common Statement of the Anglican–Methodist conversations – at least in relation to these two denominations. Many of us would also say it was evidently true for many more churches as well.

But we are left with what divides us. And these issues still make moves towards 'full visible unity' very difficult.

The divisions largely have to do with matters of oversight
- how we discipline ourselves;
- how we appoint our leaders;
- how we handle our resources of finance and buildings;
- how we take decisions about our response to the Gospel – a Gospel which in all other respects we hold in common.

In this session we look at matters of oversight and how the commitment to adjust them has to come at all levels – from local right through to national.

Our different styles of oversight and corporate decision-making contribute in turn to the formation of two distinct 'cultures' as between Methodists and Anglicans – two distinct ways of experiencing our belonging. As such they have to do with our identity, how we feel comfortable with being as we are.

But how we are, for either denomination, may not be how we need to be. Was this a lesson from Session two? The challenge may be less to do with Christian unity as such, and more about whether we dare respond to God's mission. It's back to the story of the shepherds!

'Full visible unity' between the Church of England and the Methodist Church?

The assessment of the Common Statement

1. In relation to the profession of one apostolic faith
(110) The two churches stand side by side in confessing the fundamental apostolic faith as it has been received in the orthodox Christian tradition.

2. In relation to the one baptism and one Eucharist
(138) It does not appear . . . that there are any fundamental differences of understanding between us.

3. In relation to a common ministry of word and sacraments
(176) All the essential theological ingredients to bring about an integrated ministry in the future seem to be in place . . . It should not be beyond the two churches, inspired by the Holy Spirit, to agree on the actual process of integration.

(Numbers in brackets – see p. vii)

The fourth ingredient in 'full visible unity': a common ministry of oversight (*episcopé*)

Methodists and Anglicans agree on the theory:

(167) Both of our churches believe that they are part of the one, holy catholic and apostolic Church . . . But they are clear that they are only part of the one Church . . .

(169) The life of the apostolic community of the Church – its worship, fellowship, teaching and mission – is necessarily served by an apostolic ministry . . . the Church cannot be without the ministry of the word of God and of the sacraments.

When a church recognises another church as a church belonging to the one, holy, catholic and apostolic Church of Christ, it therefore recognises the authentically apostolic nature of its ministry of word, sacrament and pastoral oversight.

Any suggestion, therefore, that a common ministry could be created by one church bestowing on another something essential to a church, that it currently lacks, would not make sense.

(175) Both the Church of England and the Methodist Church ordain, as their ordinals testify, to the ministry of the Christian Church, not merely to a denominational office. In a state of regrettable separation, each church separately intends to provide what it believes to be an apostolic ministry of word and sacrament.
This intended apostolic continuity is an expression

1. of trust in Christ's faithfulness to his Church

2. of the Church's obedience and faithfulness to the one apostolic mission.

Both churches believe that God answers their prayers. Each believes this of the other.

Two key implications

1 The Church of England can acknowledge that in another church 'the word of God is authentically preached and the sacraments of Baptism and the Eucharist are duly administered . . . as a question distinct from the question of whether that church has a ministry within the historic episcopate.' (170)

This acknowledgement has resulted in recent years in various agreements between the Church of England and churches in the Lutheran tradition – Porvoo, Meissen, Reuilly and Fetter Lane (details in Resources, p. 35). It picks up on the understanding of 'authenticity' developed in Session three and in paragraph 81 of the Common Statement.

2 However, 'full visible unity' (and an interchangeability of ministers) does require 'an ordained ministry within the historic episcopate' (171) for two reasons:

a) Anglican understanding of the representative nature of the episcopal office, which Methodists are now seen to be endorsing by 'the willingness of the Methodist Conference to become a church ordered in the historic episcopate' (174).

b) The need for consistency in relationships with Roman Catholic, Orthodox and Old Catholic churches – a concern of which Methodists and Anglicans 'are mindful' (173). This is part of a wider ecumenical consensus that ministry within the historic episcopate (with no presumptions about how it should be expressed) should be a feature of united churches.

The Methodist Conference Resolution 2000

In furtherance of the search for the visible unity of Christ's Church, the Methodist Church would willingly receive the sign of episcopal succession on the understanding that ecumenical partners sharing this sign with the Methodist Church (a) acknowledge that the latter has been and is part of the one holy catholic and apostolic Church and (b) accept that different interpretations of the precise significance of the sign exist.

'Receiving the sign of episcopal succession'

- Exactly how would Methodists acquire bishops?
- How should they 'place' them in a manner which respects their current culture and insights about what it is to be the Church?
- How would bishops in the Methodist Church sit alongside the existing bishops in the Church of England?

This is the 'further work' which will be required if the two denominations decide to proceed with the proposed Covenant.

There are plenty of caricatures of what it is to be a bishop – inside as well as outside episcopal churches! It is clear that Methodists are not being asked to accept any of these.

Methodists have already begun exploring what kind of representative 'bishop' they need in their report to Conference 2000 *Episcopé and Episcopacy*. And the House of Bishops of the Church of England has shown how Anglican thinking is developing in a wider theological context in their occasional paper *Apostolicity and Succession*.

Where do the responsibilities for oversight lie?

If we are to have a common ministry of oversight, of shared *episcopé* – and thus open the way to full visible unity – both churches will need to re-examine their traditional patterns of responsibility and decision-making. Work is already in progress, but the breakthrough may be when the two churches commit themselves to developing the new patterns together.

The Common Statement observes: 'Pastoral oversight in our two churches is exercised in **communal**, **collegial** and **personal** ways.' (181) So a great deal is already held in common. But these three strands of *episcopé*, first identified in the 1982 ecumenical document *Baptism, Eucharist and Ministry*, are 'weighted' very differently in practice. The challenge to both churches, the Common Statement concludes (193), will be to get the balance right.

The diagram below suggests that, at every 'level' between national and local, elements that are personal, collegial and communal can be identified in both traditions:

Church of England

		Personal	Collegial	Communal
England	State	Sovereign	House of Bishops	Parliament
	Church	2 Archbishops	House of Bishops	General Synod
	Diocese	Bishop	Bishop's Staff	Diocesan Synod
		Archdeacons	Bishop's Council	
	Deanery	Rural Dean	Chapter	Deanery Synod
	Parish	Incumbent		Parochial Church Council

Methodist Church of Great Britain

		Personal	Collegial	Communal
Three nations	Connexion	President	Ministerial Session at Conference	Conference
			District Chairs' Meeting	
	District	Chairman		District Synod
	Circuit	Superintendent Minister	Stewards	Circuit Meeting
	Church	Minister in Pastoral Charge	Stewards	Church Council

The task is to get the balance right.

(193) Personal *episcopé* in both churches is exercised in a collegial and communal context.

Anglicans and Methodists are re-examining the balance between personal, collegial and communal expressions of oversight.

For example, the Methodist Church is currently considering how personal oversight is exercised and whether that might change or develop and the Church of England is exploring what collaborative ministry involves at all levels of the Church's life.

Superficially similar

The two systems operate, however, in very different ways:

1 There is a mismatch as to where the weight of responsibility lies.

For Methodists it tends to lie at the national level with Conference or at circuit level with the superintendent minister.

For the Church of England it lies at the diocesan level with the bishop and at the local level with the incumbent.

How then can like talk with like at any level? Degrees of responsibility differ as well as whether the responsibility is exercised individually or corporately.

2 More broadly in terms of influence in decision-making, the Church of England appears relatively top-heavy and the Methodists bottom-heavy.

This is despite the fact that the authority vested in Conference means that Methodism is more centralized than the Church of England, where the 44 dioceses are largely autonomous.

3 The two 'gaps' in the collegiate column may be significant.

In Methodism at district level – although some districts are moving towards staff teams and a greater role for the District Policy Committee and there is talk of devolving some connexional funds to be administered by districts.

In the Church of England at parish level – although some parishes are moving to greater collegiality through 'local ministry' schemes, etc.

A common understanding that drives us to find a unified *episcopé*

(178) Our ecclesiologies are not compatible with separate, parallel structures of oversight between churches that were already united in doctrine, sacraments and pastoral ministry, except as a temporary anomaly on the way to full visible unity.

(180) The covenantal agreement between our two churches that these Formal Conversations propose, would justify formal arrangements for shared oversight, as a stage on the way to a single, unified *episcopé*.

**Parallel structures?
But still separate?
A temporary anomaly?**

Can a Covenant commitment take us forward beyond these?

Find out more in the final session!

Insights from the Bible

On a common ministry of oversight (as offered in the Common Statement paragraph 177)

- The Church lives under the authority of Christ its Head (Colossians 1.18)
- and is led into all the truth by the Holy Spirit through the Word of God (John 16.13).
- In each generation it has to seek the mind of Christ (Philippians 2.5) and
- to be receptive to the guidance of the Spirit' (Galatians 5.16,25).

(177) The Church is a fellowship (*koinonia*) of those baptised into the royal priesthood of Jesus Christ. All baptised believers share in the threefold messianic office of Christ who is Prophet, Priest and King. Participating in his royal priesthood, Christians share in the governance of his Church.

'Heroes' and 'Hijackers'

Different Christian traditions all have their heroes. Typically Methodists relate in this way to the Wesleys, as Lutherans do to Martin Luther etc. Intriguingly Anglicans do not feel the same way about, for example, Thomas Cranmer.

The danger comes when we assume that our heroes can do no wrong. At that point heroes too easily become 'hijackers', because they draw our attention away from Christ.

At a time when all churches are struggling to find gospel relevance, new heroes and new hijackers are easy to find – heroes when they are true to Christ, hijackers when they offer tempting, even life-threatening, short-cuts along the costly road of discipleship.

A common ministry of *episcopé* is about holding Christ's Body together in the face of these temptations. And for every individual disciple there is a corresponding ministry of 'followership'.

The heroes, and the hijackers, are not just those with a national or international profile. They can just as well be your local leaders, ordained or lay, in your local church or even in an individual house-group.

The challenge is to listen to one another when one person's hero is seen by another to be a hijacker, because both perceptions could be nearly true!

Session five
Programme for group work

Working out how to live as one Body in Christ

Group leaders should check in advance that they have the facts available about how Methodists and Anglicans (and other denominations) are organized locally.

- Recall lessons from the fourth session.
- In twos and threes (either mixed or by denomination) look back at the stereotypes identified in Session one and the 'demons' named in Session two. After reading the notes for this session, you may recognize other stereotypes – about vicars and bishops, about Methodist ministers, about those regarded as 'heroes' or 'hijackers' in each tradition (see below left).
- Compare results in the full group. To what extent do these reflect a mutual ignorance about how different denominations actually operate and what it feels like to be a member of one of these denominations 'from the inside'?
- **Either:**
  find out about how the different denominations operate locally and about the level of contact between clergy and ministers in your area. Do they share their aspirations and concerns, pray regularly together, dream dreams together – and actively support each other? What prevents it happening? And what would happen if they did?
- **Or:**
  using the Bible passages in the left-hand column, begin to list the characteristics of what it is to live as one Body in Christ. What are the essential ingredients that allow us to recognize that a group of people is part of the one Church of Christ? What features that we usually associate with 'church' are in fact incidental?
- What steps must we take before we reach the point where it is taken for granted that we each need the other (and the insights and active involvement of other Christian traditions) if we are to be faithful to God's mission?
- Offer your thoughts to God in prayer and thankfulness for his overriding reconciling love.

Suggestions for prayer, worship, feedback and follow-up are provided on pp. 31–2.

An exercise for those who think they know the system!

The diagrams on page 19 illustrate the structure of the Church of England and of the Methodist Church. See what conclusions you draw by colouring in the boxes, and then contrasting the two churches:

- Legal responsibility   red
- Delegated responsibility   blue
- Highly influential   green
- Limited responsibility   yellow

NB Even if you end up with multi-coloured boxes, the question might then be which boxes have the largest amounts of red or blue!

Session six: Covenant
God's bow in the clouds
Seven affirmations and six commitments – a 'covenant' relationship

'Made in heaven'

The original mandate for the conversations looked to an outcome that would produce a Declaration and a Commitment which the Church of England and the Methodist Church could make, binding them to a new relationship. What is proposed is a 'Covenant'.

The concept of a Covenant is deeply biblical and well understood by many churches in the Reformed tradition.

Making a Covenant is not a light undertaking. The affirmations and commitments that go with it are not optional extras but will only be seen to be fulfilled if they fundamentally influence the life, outlook and styles of operation of both churches.

At one level the **affirmations** say nothing new, but they do have historic significance:

1. They are mutual – each church affirming the same about the other.

2. They overwrite stereotypes and misunderstandings that the churches have had about each other that have been accumulated from the past, and which sadly can still sometimes be heard today.

(Part of the purpose of the group work suggested in this book is to enable people to get these negative impressions and feelings into the open, and then to find the courage and the trust to move on together, consigning the rubbish to the waste bin!)

The **commitments** specifically deal with the remaining items on the 'practical' agenda which have to be attended to on the road to 'full visible unity'. It is worth noting that for Anglicans, every one of the commitments is already legally possible under Canon B 43.

How long it takes to settle these things depends on how preoccupied we are with our denominational survival, or how ready we are to 'make the transition' and become caught up in what God is doing in God's world in the name of Jesus Christ and for the sake of God's kingdom. The co-chairmen of the conversations, in their foreword to the report, call for the churches to implement the terms of the Covenant 'with all speed'.

Meanwhile these national proposals also represent a challenge more locally: what covenant are you prepared to make with your brothers and sisters in Christ at the levels in which you are engaged so that God's love can be made known in God's world?

Insights from the Bible

In the shadow of a rainbow . . .

■ God's Covenant with Noah after the flood was his 'bow in the clouds' (Genesis 9.13).

■ A rainbow seems to symbolize the unity in diversity in God's creation.

■ And a rainbow has no shadow!

■ Both St Paul (Galatians 3 and 4 and elsewhere) and the writer to the Hebrews (Chapters 7 – 10) associate Christ's new community of disciples, his Church, as inheritors of God's Covenant with Abraham ('the father of many nations').

■ Christ's New Covenant is presented as being in stark contrast with the 'Old' Covenant through Moses (e.g. 2 Corinthians 3.12-18).

■ In fact the writer to the Hebrews goes back even before Abraham to Melchizedek and then emphasizes the everlasting nature of the New Covenant relationship which is ours with God because of Jesus Christ.

If there's one lesson to be learned about covenants, it is that they are not just human agreements.

Like marriages, covenants are 'made in heaven'.
They are made with God.
They are made by God.

Covenants may be needed at many levels

1. Local covenants

Perhaps it is time to rethink the traditional Local Ecumenical Partnership. Local covenants can exist in many new guises.

What would a covenant look like

between a small group of churches in a defined locality, if your goal was 'a single Christian presence', while still being as multi-coloured as a rainbow?

2. Deanery – circuit covenants

Deaneries and circuits often cover similar areas, and the number of Anglican and Methodist congregations often greatly exceeds the number of other denominations, especially in more rural areas.

What would a covenant look like

for a 'mission partnership' between deanery and circuit in your area?

An example

from North Lincolnshire is described in some detail in *Releasing Energy* (see p. 34). Two lessons can already be learned from their experience:

■ We should not fear bi-lateral covenants. Churches from other traditions in North Lincolnshire are discovering they have their own special part to play. They trigger new initiatives; they host joint activity. They make things possible in situations where neither partner wants to take the first step and be accused of seeking to dominate.

■ Partnerships at this level need not 'force the pace' more locally or prescribe ill-fitting standardized solutions. Unique localities continue to need unique solutions. The wider partnership provides the 'climate of presumption' which encourages people to feel that local solutions are worth the effort.

3. Diocese – district covenants

Diocesan synods and district synods have held joint meetings in many places. But the real decision-making in both denominations tends to be done beforehand – at the Bishop's Council, or in the District Policy Committee.

What would a covenant look like

between the 'real' decision-makers in district and diocese – and how could they exercise it to achieve really integrated strategic planning based on shared resources and the needs of the wider community? Since the Church of England deploys most of its resources for ministry and mission at diocesan level, well-thought-out practical commitments to partnership in mission at this level could well do more than anything else to change the culture and enable the two churches to grow into unity.

A 'climate of presumption' at every level?

If the same spirit of commitment could be achieved at every level, then both denominations might recognize merits in each other's systems – for the sake of a more effective and faithful engagement with God's mission. They might even feel more positive about convergence that is already happening, e.g.

● Some Anglican dioceses are already wanting to devolve greater responsibility to deaneries, both for mission strategy and for the effective deployment of resources. What might this do to the parson's 'freehold'?

● Methodists in turn, having expressed agreement about their willingness to accept bishops, are needing to think about how a representative personal episcopacy might help serve God's mission, perhaps especially at district level.

Two barriers to be overcome

1. Ecumenical geography – a bigger barrier than we think!

If Methodists and Anglicans are going to work effectively together at many levels, there is real urgency to sort out the long-recognized problem of 'ecumenical geography'.

As usual God may be using external drivers to make it happen. On this occasion 'Cyrus' (cf. Isaiah 45) may well be the increasing regionalization of government in England.

Already we should be taking more account of secular boundaries, e.g. local authority boundaries or travel-to-work areas, when re-shaping deaneries and circuits, even if it means clustering deaneries and circuits rather than merging them.

Then at the head of each cluster, on behalf of both, or even all, churches, how about appointing a full-time ecumenical moderator to be both rural dean and superintendent minister (and acknowledged leader of the Church in mission) – as already happens in Milton Keynes?

In this, as in so many things, the challenge is to risk what is familiar (and working well enough) in favour of something that might eventually be better.

2. Cultural differences that reflect divisions in wider society

The problem seems to be that Methodists and members of the Church of England have, at least in living memory, reflected slightly different social backgrounds. The Church of England has often appeared to be more 'Tory', the Methodists more 'Socialist'. In some places it could come down to whether tea or coffee is served after the Sunday morning service!

Like so much else, these are stereotypes, and might well be just not true in your locality! Dealing with them will always require sensitivity – a generous spirit of awareness. Otherwise they will continue to bite us when we least expect it!

An Anglican–Methodist Covenant

We, the Methodist Church of Great Britain and the Church of England, on the basis of

- our shared history,
- our full agreement in the apostolic faith,
- our shared theological understandings of the nature and mission of the Church and of its ministry and oversight,
- and our agreement on the goal of full visible unity, as set out in the previous sections of our Common Statement,

hereby make the following Covenant in the form of interdependent Affirmations and Commitments.

We do so

- both in a spirit of penitence for all that human sinfulness and narrowness of vision have contributed to our past divisions,
- believing that we have been impoverished through our separation and that our witness to the gospel has been weakened accordingly,
- and in a spirit of thanksgiving and joy for the convergence in faith and collaboration in mission that we have experienced in recent years.

Affirmations

1. We affirm one another's churches as true churches belonging to the One, Holy, Catholic and Apostolic Church of Jesus Christ and as truly participating in the apostolic mission of the whole people of God.

2. We affirm that in both our churches the word of God is authentically preached, and the sacraments of Baptism and the Eucharist are duly administered and celebrated.

3. We affirm that both our churches confess in word and life the apostolic faith revealed in the Holy Scriptures and set forth in the ecumenical Creeds.

4. We affirm that one another's ordained and lay ministries are given by God as instruments of God's grace, to build up the people of God in faith, hope and love, for the ministry of word, sacrament and pastoral care and to share in God's mission in the world.

5. We affirm that one another's ordained ministries possess both the inward call of the Holy Spirit and Christ's commission given through the Church.

6. We affirm that both our churches embody the conciliar, connexional nature of the Church and that communal, collegial and personal oversight (episkopé) is exercised within them in various forms.

7. We affirm that there already exists a basis for agreement on the principles of episcopal oversight as a visible sign and instrument of the communion of the Church in time and space.

Commitments

1. We commit ourselves, as a priority, to work to overcome the remaining obstacles to the organic unity of our two churches, on the way to the full visible unity of Christ's Church. In particular, we look forward to the time when the fuller visible unity of our churches makes possible a united, interchangeable ministry.

2. We commit ourselves to realise more deeply our common life and mission and to share the distinctive contributions of our traditions, taking steps to bring about closer collaboration in all areas of witness and service in our needy world.

3. We commit ourselves to continue to welcome each other's baptised members to participate in the fellowship, worship and mission of our churches.

4. We commit ourselves to encourage forms of eucharistic sharing, including eucharistic hospitality, in accordance with the rules of our respective churches.

5. We commit ourselves to listen to each other and to take account of each other's concerns, especially in areas that affect our relationship as churches.

6. We commit ourselves to continue to develop structures of joint or shared communal, collegial and personal oversight, including shared consultation and decision-making, on the way to a fully united ministry of oversight.

The joys and the frustrations!

Over the years many have become frustrated at our human failure to resolve our differences. Denominational leaders encourage us to take risks, but no-one seems able to identify a risk that we might be allowed to take!

Equally there is a frustration because so many of our church members seem to have little desire to share this life-giving experience of the Spirit.

Outfaced by mission – rather than unity!

But people may not be opposed to Christian unity as such. Unity would certainly be lovely if it was on my terms! It is just that most us rather like our churches as they are because they meet our spiritual needs – and woe betide us if they didn't!

But if maintaining our comfort zones is our only concern, we have fatally missed God's call to serve God's mission in God's world. Once we catch this sense of urgency (and don't substitute for it a lust for our mission on behalf of our church) we soon see how essential it is to express God's reconciling love through full visible unity. But it is the unity of the rainbow – God's life-affirming bow in the clouds.

The goal at the local level is 'a single (dynamically loving) Christian presence' in every place. And the challenge to Christian disciples of all traditions in a particular place is to enable others to recognize the Good News of God's love for them through Jesus Christ through whatever windows of spiritual insight and practical engagement our different traditions can offer them.

The core message of the Common Statement from these Anglican–Methodist conversations is precisely that mission and unity are inseparable.

But this is not just something to be deduced theoretically from Scripture. It is precisely that powerful and palpable *koinonia* of the Holy Spirit that we are invited to experience on the ground – if only we didn't keep putting obstacles in the way of God's purposes because of our selfish preoccupations!

Session six
Programme for group work

● Recall lessons from the fifth session.

● Individual group members should check out privately whether they are able to make each of the seven affirmations.

● The full group can then explore the areas where doubt remains – perhaps by consulting the full text of the Common Statement.

● The question then facing the group is this: What steps should we be taking to give practical effect to the six commitments if we apply them at our own 'level'?

● How can we implement these commitments
  ● as individuals – lay or ordained?
  ● in our small groups?
  ● in the corporate life of our congregations?

  What elements might we want to include in a possible covenant in our locality? Who should it involve and what would be its scope? What is the first step we must take to get the process started?

● At this point there might be further work the group wants to do to plan how these thoughts can be addressed in the workshop day, if one is being organized.

● More than anything else, however, by this stage in the process, the priority is prayer. Covenants are made with God. Covenants are made by God.

Suggestions for prayer, worship, feedback and follow-up are provided on pp. 32–3.

A timetable for the Covenant

June and July 2002: debate on the Covenant proposals in the Methodist Conference and the Church of England General Synod.

Subsequent twelve months: likely referral for discussion through both Churches. Over this period of discussion, responses and reflections also invited from partner Churches.

June and July 2003: proposals return to Conference and General Synod for approval.

After approval:

1. A joint Implementation Commission, to ensure that the Covenant is made real in the lives of our churches.
2. Further conversations to consider the outstanding theological issues.

An optional workshop
Finding our local priorities

From memories to mission
– laying the foundations for a common agenda
– the first steps towards a local covenant?

Sharing a vision with your congregations

Throughout the six sessions of this study guide, the insights and concerns of the Common Statement on the formal Anglican–Methodist conversations have been set alongside the local scene.

Those taking part in the conversations are clearly excited by a vision – the possibility of two UK churches growing into full visible unity as they adapt themselves to be more effectively part of God's mission, signs of God's reconciling love in a fragmented society.

The suggestions on these pages for an optional workshop, as a follow-up to the small group studies, are intended to give all the members of your local churches a chance to glimpse that vision for themselves. The workshop could lead to more dramatic outcomes (but see below).

Two key ingredients make up the workshop, the first of which needs work to be done in advance. The activities can involve every member of the congregation.

A   Looking at ourselves in context
    1. A local map
    2. A time chart

B   Putting *koinonia* into practice

Full details can be found on the next two pages.

Who do we want to come to the workshop?

The aim is to gather as many members as possible from the congregations of all the churches represented at the study groups. If the workshop is to do more than help a wider a group of church members to catch a vision, the Methodist Church Council and the Parochial Church Council will need to give it their backing from the start and be ready to work with any outcomes.

■ The arrangements proposed on these pages assume around 50 participants.

■ A neutral venue such as a school might be appropriate.

Pros and cons of when to hold a workshop

1 A separate full day event on a Saturday

Saturdays give the most time, but people may be reluctant to give up a whole day.

2 A Sunday event after morning service and lasting into the afternoon

Sundays will draw larger numbers but there will be less time. Special arrangements will also have to be made for a joint act of worship that morning between the participating churches. A great idea – except, of course, that we know this means that some will stay away!

3 Two evenings in successive weeks

Two evenings give barely enough time – with the added risk that the same people will not attend both weeks! But for some, this may be the only option in a busy diary.

Whichever option you choose, pick a date at least three months ahead and start preparing for it now!

A Looking at ourselves in context

Two activities to be tackled in advance of the workshop

A1 The local map

Some details of what can be done with a local map have already been given on p. 12.

However, when the map is used in preparation for the workshop, there are other possibilities.

The process

In each church arrange to display a detailed map of the area showing street names if possible.

Highlight the main features and routes people use as suggested on p. 12.

But in addition, invite every member of the congregation to mark (with a pin or coloured adhesive disc) where they live. If they are off the map, place the marker at the end of the road along which they travel to reach church.

This then provides some evidence in relation to the questions about church membership posed on p. 12.

For suggestions on how to review the results of these two activities during the course of the workshop, see p. 28.

A2 A time chart

Working towards a common view of our local histories

Creating a time chart is potentially a useful exercise in any congregation, because it allows people to be reminded of how God has been with them on their journey and how, in fact, church life does not stand still, however much we wish it would!

The chart will often explain why things are as they are, why certain suggestions for change and development meet unexpectedly strong resistance. In other words it can often pinpoint the reasons for insecurity. Making the chart is good fun and can involve church members of every age.

The Process

In each church in your locality arrange to have a large sheet of paper along a wall. The sheet will be divided into sections with a scale of dates along the bottom. Because we are looking at the Common Statement of the recent Anglican-Methodist conversations it might be worth starting the map as far back as 1750 showing fifty-year intervals to 1900, twenty-year intervals until 1940, ten-year intervals until 1990 and smaller divisions (as appropriate) to date.

All members of the congregation are invited to note on the sheet, according to the date, significant events they can think of that took place at that time.

If people can produce photos, press cuttings, programmes or orders of service, this is bound to create a lot of interest.

The fascinating stage is when each church brings its display to a central location where church members from the different churches can see each other's story and discuss what lessons can be learned.

Possible questions

1. To what extent are these the private stories of self-contained congregations and to what extent the common story of the local community?

2. How has each congregation changed over the years? Have there been significant shifts in policy, in the way the church does things? Have there been major crises, or hard times when dreams were unfulfilled?

3. What evidence is there for changing attitudes between the churches?

4. Have any churches had previous experience of division or re-unification? How did it work out? How does it affect the present situation?

5. Have there been major events in the local community, which have affected how the local churches have understood their role?

6. In all these stories, where was God?

1750	1800	1850	1900	1920	1940	1950	1960	1970	1980	1990	1992	1994	1996	1998	1999	2000	2001

B Putting *koinonia* into practice

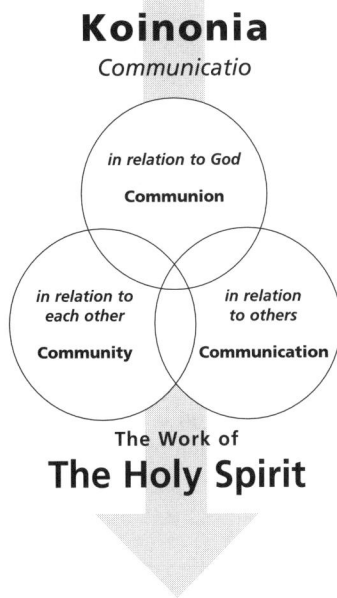

Koinonia
Communicatio

in relation to God
Communion

in relation to
each other
Community

in relation
to others
Communication

The Work of
The Holy Spirit

(See p. 38 for expanded photocopiable version.)

A key quotation from the Common Statement

(92) Because mission is essential to the Church's nature it follows that it must be related to the four dimensions of the Church that we confess in the Nicene Creed: unity, holiness, catholicity and apostolicity. Mission and unity once again prove to be inseparable.

But it is not only the '**oneness**' of the Church that shapes its mission.

Its **holiness** means that it is 'set apart' by God's calling and election to serve God's purpose of righteousness and peace and must reflect those attributes of God in its own life.

Its **catholicity** means that it aims to hold together the rich diversity of gifts and insights generated by the breadth of Christian response throughout many cultures. Diverse expressions of the gospel answer to the diversity of human needs and situations. Such diversity can therefore enhance mission.

Finally, the Church's **apostolicity** means that it is sent into the world in intentional continuity with the mission of the Apostles, with their preaching of the apostolic gospel and teaching of the apostolic faith.

All four dimensions of the Church – its unity, holiness, catholicity and apostolicity – require visible expression.

Three relationships
all energized by the Holy Spirit

The theological language of *koinonia*, as it is used in the Common Statement to explain the 'mission' basis for the search for Christian unity, can seem pretty abstract and generalized. The ideas stand a better chance of 'coming alive' and engaging our passions if we can use them as a yardstick for our local church life.

The second half of the suggested workshop day is built round an exercise which offers local Christian communities a fresh way to see the 'shape' of their local church life and begin to discern priorities in response to God's mission.

We believe in		Koinonia =	
In relation to	One		
God	Holy	Communion +	Faith +
Each other	Catholic and	Community +	Community +
Others	Apostolic	Communication	Action
	Church		

A single act of divine love – enabling three relationships

In the Vulgate (the Latin Bible) *koinonia* is usually translated *communicatio*, a word which has three close cognates in English:

- **communion** – our relationship with God
- **community** – our relationship with fellow disciples
- **communication** – our relationship with the rest of God's world

'We believe in one, holy, catholic and apostolic church'

- Our *communion* with God is what characterizes us as **holy**.
- Our *community* with fellow disciples is what characterizes us as **catholic**.
- Our *communication* with the rest of God's world is what characterizes us as **apostolic**.

Yet it is the **one** energy of the Holy Spirit that makes possible this single dynamic experience of *koinonia*.

Essential ingredients

For too long we have allowed the church to be shaped by finance and traditional structures. We have been trapped in a mindset which can only envisage 'church' made up of **minister + building + stipend**. If any one of these three is taken away, traditional congregational life falters.

In how many ways could we envisage 'church' if its main ingredients (based on the Holy Spirit's *koinonia*) were **faith + community + action**?

A programme for the workshop

designed for a free-standing all day event

The time charts and local maps from the different churches need to be displayed around the main room where the workshop is to be held. Also on display should be the feedback from the study group sessions.

A large screen and OHP will be useful for plenary sessions. Flip chart paper and pens will be needed when people work in smaller groups.

10 a.m. As people arrive, they should be offered coffee, etc. and a sheet of paper with questions (see next column). They should then be invited to view the displays and make a note of their reactions.

10.45 a.m. Worship and prayer (see p. 32 for ideas).

11 a.m. Plenary: collect people's reactions to the displays under the three headings suggested on the guidance sheet by inviting people to call out their comments. Check how far others agree, and then log the comment on the OHP.

NB: Avoid too much debate. The trick is to allow just enough debate to register the issue! Those who had previously taken part in the study groups should look for connections between the issues raised and the six themes of the group work: perceptions, history, mission, an ordered faith, oversight and covenant.

12 noon (approx!) Review the lists and try highlighting the biggest issues under each heading.

12.30 p.m. Break for lunch. Encourage people to share their lunch break with others they don't already know.

1.30 p.m. Introduce the idea of three intersecting circles of relationship, with an explanation of *koinonia* based on the material on p. 27. An OHP transparency can be made from the full-page version of the three circles diagram (see p. 40).

2 p.m. Invite people to locate the issues highlighted before lunch within the three circles of relationship and then prepare people for work in small groups.

2.20 p.m. Small groups of no more than 8 people should be invited to focus their attention on the issues raised within just one of the three circles of relationship. Participants in the study groups should be spread around the groups but may not be best employed as group leaders.

The key question facing the groups is: **As we think about the issues raised within this circle of relationship, what will we do (or not do!) if we are experiencing the Holy Spirit's *koinonia*?** Possible answers should be listed under four headings:

1. Things to continue (and thank God for).
2. Things to stop (either to repent of or acknowledge they have outlived their relevance).
3. Things to do now.
4. Things to plan or campaign for.

3 p.m. In a final plenary session, gather up the comments made by the groups on a matrix (see next column). The completed matrix can then be typed up for further study and reflection within the local churches and in other joint planning groups.

3.45 p.m. End the day with thanksgiving, commitment, song (!) and the Grace (see next column).

Guidance sheet as people view the displays

(See p. 39 for expanded photocopiable version.)

As you view the displays and read the feedback, **compare the churches.** On the time charts, look out for:

- Different ways the stories are told: Do they tell the story of the church or of the community?
- The effect of what happened on church life.
- When churches cooperated (or didn't!).
- Anything unusual.

On the local maps, look out for:

- Areas where there are no churchgoers.
- Where church members come from (differences between the churches).
- The 'disadvantaged' parts of your area.

Make notes on this sheet under three headings:

1. Pleasant surprises.
2. Things that concern or disturb you.
3. Needs or opportunities that occur to you.

Matrix for the final session of the workshop

Comments recorded here may well form the basis for a set of priorities and a common agenda for engaging in God's mission – perhaps a first step towards a local covenant.

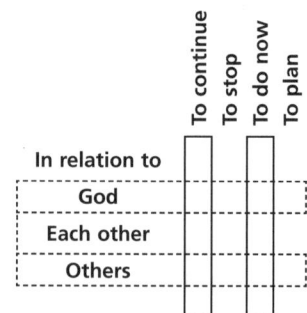

In relation to	To continue	To stop	To do now	To plan
God				
Each other				
Others				

Let's say 'The Grace' together . . .

At the end of our meetings we are used to blessing one another with the words: 'The grace of our Lord Jesus Christ, the love of God and the fellowship (koinonia) of the Holy Spirit . . .'

Yet these are not merely blessings from God which we receive. Grace, love and 'fellowship' (see p. 27 for the real meaning of this word!) are mission words, life-giving activity by God through us for the sake of all his creation.

Once that tingle of realization runs through us, we'll never be able to say these words the same way again!

Worship
A faithful response

These pages offer a selection of resources for shared prayer and worship at each of the six group sessions. They are not intended for use as a set liturgy.

Session one
Perceptions

A psalm
Psalm 139: God knows us
A prayerful way of reading the psalms is when each person round a circle reads a verse in turn.

To ponder
1. The mismatch between self-image (which might include our denominational identity) and self-knowledge.
2. The mismatch between our knowledge of God and God's knowledge of us.

A prayer of penitence
Come, let us return to the Lord and say:

Lord our God,
in our sin we have avoided
   your call.
Our love for you is like a
   morning cloud,
like the dew that goes away early.
Have mercy on us;
deliver us from judgement;
bind up our wounds
and revive us;
in Jesus Christ our Lord. Amen.

Hosea 6

A hymn
1. Will you come and follow me
   if I but call your name?
   Will you go where you
      don't know,
   and never be the same?
   Will you let my love be shown,
   will you let my name be known,
   will you let my life be grown
   in you, and you in me?

2. Will you leave yourself behind
   if I but call your name?
   Will you care for cruel and kind,
   and never be the same?
   Will you risk the hostile stare
   should your life attract or scare,
   will you let me answer prayer
   in you, and you in me?

3. Will you let the blinded see
   if I but call your name?
   Will you set the pris'ners free,
   and never be the same?
   Will you kiss the leper clean
   and do such as this unseen,
   and admit to what I mean
   in you, and you in me?

4. Will you love the 'you' you hide
   if I but call your name?
   Will you quell the fear inside,
   and never be the same?
   Will you use the faith
      you've found
   to reshape the world around
   through my sight and touch
      and sound
   in you, and you in me?

5. Lord, your summons echoes true
   when you but call my name.
   Let me turn and follow you,
   and never be the same.
   In your company I'll go
   where your love and
      footsteps show.
   Thus I'll move and live and
      grow
   in you, and you in me.

A prayer of commitment
God of compassion,
through your Son Jesus Christ
you have reconciled your
   people to yourself.
As we follow his example
of prayer and fasting,
may we obey you with willing
hearts
and serve one another in holy love;
through Jesus Christ our Lord.

Feedback to the congregations
The best thing we can do about our misperceptions of each other is laugh about them. Do you remember what you looked like when you stood in front of those crazy distorting mirrors at the fairground?
Can members of the group put together a dialogue caricaturing a spoof meeting between a 'typical' Anglican and a 'typical' Methodist? Try it out on your congregations and then mount the best punch lines on a display at the back of each church!

Action
Visit the oldest 'resident' members of each other's congregations (i.e. the life-long worshippers at that church) and hear their reminiscences!

Session two
History

A psalm
Psalm 40: God loves us

To ponder
Throughout all the confusions of our divided histories, Christians of every tradition have known God's constant love – a stream of life-giving water welling up both in familiar and in unexpected places.

Have we been too defensive or possessive in response to God's generosity? Have we been too concerned to put a fence round our favourite well, rather than share the water with others?

A prayer of penitence
Have mercy on me, O God,
in your constant love;
in the fullness of your mercy
blot out my offences.

Wash away all my guilt,
and cleanse me from my sin.
Create in me a clean heart,
   O God,
and renew a right spirit
   within me.
Give me the joy of your
   help again
and strengthen me with
   a willing spirit.

Psalm 51

A hymn

1. Christ, our King before creation,
   Life, before all life began,
   Crowned in deep humiliation
   By your partners in God's plan,
   Make us humble in believing,
   And, believing, bold to pray:
   'Lord, forgive our self-deceiving,
   Come and reign in us today!'

2. Lord of time and Lord of history,
   Giving, when the world despairs,
   Faith to wrestle with the mystery
   Of a God who loves and cares,
   Make us humble in believing,
   And, believing, bold to pray:
   'Lord, by grace beyond
       conceiving,
   Come and reign in us today!'

3. Word that ends our long
       debating,
   Life of God which sets us free,
   Through your body recreating
   Life as life is meant to be,
   Make us humble in believing,
   And, believing, bold to pray:
   'Lord, in us your aim achieving,
   Come and reign in us today!'

A prayer of commitment

In faith we pray to God,
who is more ready to hear than
we are to ask.

Let us pray for the whole Church
   of God,
that, rejoicing in our richness
   and variety,
we may seek peace and unity
and be constantly renewed for
   mission and service.

Silence

The Lord hears our prayer.
Thanks be to God.

Feedback to the congregations

Introduce people to the angels
and demons – both as we view
the churches as they are and as
we try to visualize the Church God
is already bringing about. Collate
the responses people put on their
worksheets and invite penitence
for past failures and present fears.

Action

Find out where people are already
experiencing 'new ways of being
church' and arrange to visit them.

Session three
Mission

A psalm
Psalm 96: God reigns!

To ponder

In what ways is God already
at work in our local area?
In what ways and through
whom are people discovering
God's healing love – even if they
cannot yet recognize God's hand
in it or name Jesus Christ?

A prayer of penitence

O King enthroned on high,
filling the earth with your glory:
holy is your name,
Lord God almighty.
In our sinfulness we cry to you
to take our guilt away,
and to cleanse our lips to speak
   your word,
through Jesus Christ our Lord.

A hymn

1. From heav'n you came, helpless
       babe,
   entered our world, your glory
       veiled;
   not to be served but to serve,
   and give your life that we might
       live.

   This is our God, the Servant King,
   he calls us now to follow him,
   to bring our lives as a daily
       offering
   of worship to the Servant King.

2. There in the garden of tears,
   my heavy load he chose to bear;
   his heart with sorrow was torn.
   'Yet not my will but yours,'
       he said.

3. Come see his hands and his feet,
   the scars that speak of sacrifice,
   hands that flung stars into space,
   to cruel nails surrendered.

4. So let us learn how to serve,
   and in our lives enthrone him;
   each other's needs to prefer,
   for it is Christ we're serving.

Extract from the song 'The Servant King'
by Graham Kendrick. Copyright © 1983
Thankyou Music.

The washing of feet

If possible, a group might choose to
perform this important sacramental
act together.

Gracious God,
your Son Jesus Christ girded
   himself with a towel
and washed the feet of his disciples.
Give us the will to be the servants
   of others
as he was the servant of all,
who gave up his life and died for us,
yet lives and reigns with you and
   the Holy Spirit,
one God, now and for ever.

Feedback to the congregations

Either:
introduce the proposal for a
workshop including the plans
for a time chart and local map
in each church;

Or:
show the results of work done
by the group using a local map –
and the questions it poses.

Action

'Prayer-walk' your local area, but
also take a camera and make up
a series of slides (or a *PowerPoint*
presentation) for use as a
meditation in the course of worship.

Session four
An ordered faith

A psalm
Psalm 119: God teaches us

NB This psalm is in 22 sections each starting with a different letter of the Hebrew alphabet. Choose one or two of your favourite sections e.g. those starting at verses 33, 41, 97, 105 or 169.

To ponder
So often we try to comfort ourselves by putting boundaries around truth. It is so reassuring if we can put up a fence within which we can say we are right – and everyone outside is wrong.

Yet maybe God's truth, beyond our understanding, is 'centred' truth, not 'bounded' truth, a truth to which we are drawn as we become 'centred' on God.

Our belief is 'in' God not 'about' God.

A prayer of penitence

Jesus Christ, risen Master and
    triumphant Lord,
we come to you in sorrow for
    our sins,
and confess to you our weakness
    and unbelief.

We have lived by our own strength,
and not by the power of your
    resurrection.
In your mercy, forgive us.
Lord, hear us and help us.

We have lived by the light of
    our own eyes,
as faithless and not believing.
In your mercy, forgive us.
Lord, hear us and help us.

We have lived for this world alone,
and doubted our home in heaven.
In your mercy, forgive us.
Lord, hear us and help us.

A hymn
1. Christ is the world's light,
    he and none other;
   Born in our darkness,
    he became our brother.
   If we have seen him, we have
    seen the Father:
   Glory to God on high.

2. Christ is the world's peace,
    he and none other;
   No one can serve him and
    despise another;
   Who else unites us,
    one in God the Father?
   Glory to God on high.

3. Christ is the world's Life,
    he and none other;
   Sold once for silver,
    murdered here, our brother –
   He, who redeems us,
    reigns with God the Father:
   Glory to God on high.

4. Give God the glory,
    God and none other;
   Give God the glory, Spirit,
    Son and Father;
   Give God the glory,
    God in man my brother:
   Glory to God on high.

The Nicene Creed
The group could read it aloud together, taking care to ponder its meaning. The full text is on p. 33.

A prayer of commitment
Now that we have been put right with God through faith,
we have peace with God through our Lord Jesus Christ.

He has brought us by faith into the grace of God.
We rejoice in the hope of sharing God's glory!
This hope does not deceive us:
for God has poured his love into our hearts by the gift of his Spirit.
Romans 5.1-2

Feedback to the congregations
Might it be worth asking a congregation to express their preferences as follows?

   a) *Who gets most excited about what they already know of God's love?*
   b) *Who gets most excited about what they don't yet know?*
Both responses are entirely appropriate, but you might also have to ask:
   c) *Who doesn't relate to either question?*

The range of responses might provide an opening for introducing people to the group's reactions to their experience of working through Session four, especially the final set of four questions. Responses to these four questions should be included on a display for use at the workshop.

Action
Those representing your church on denominational synods etc. perhaps need to be briefed to keep a sense of proportion when debating the mass of detail in this section of the Common Statement. Truth is not something that any of us 'possesses'.

Session five
Oversight

A psalm
Psalm 23: God cherishes us

To ponder
Reflect on the evident truth across the Christian traditions (and down the centuries) that the loving hand of God has been at work in the hearts and lives of Christians even when they disagree about doctrine, or the way they order their church life, and even when they deny each other's right to be called a disciple of Jesus Christ!

A prayer of penitence
Gracious and holy God,
we confess that we have sinned against you and against our
    neighbour.
Your Spirit gives light,
 but we have preferred darkness;
your Spirit gives wisdom,
 but we have been foolish;
your Spirit gives power,
 but we have trusted in our
    own strength.
For the sake of Jesus Christ, your
    Son,
forgive our sins,
and enable us by your Spirit
to serve you in joyful obedience,
to the glory of your Name. Amen.

A hymn
1. Father, hear the prayer we offer:
    not for ease that prayer shall be,
   but for strength that we may
    ever live our lives courageously.

2. Not for ever in green pastures
   do we ask our way to be;
   but the steep and rugged
   pathway may we tread rejoicingly.

3. Not for ever by still waters
   would we idly rest and stay;
   but would smite the living
      fountains
   from the rocks along our way.

4. Be our strength in hours
      of weakness,
   in our wanderings be our guide;
   through endeavour, failure,
      danger,
   Father, be thou at our side.

The Great Commission
2 Corinthians 4.5-10, quoted below, is part of a set reading in the Church of England's Order for the Ordination or Consecration of a Bishop. Bishop Lesslie Newbigin identified it as St Paul's version of 'The Great Commission', a title usually given to Matthew 28.19.

It is not ourselves that we proclaim; we proclaim Christ Jesus as Lord, and ourselves as your servants, for Jesus' sake. For the same God who said, 'Out of darkness let light shine', has caused his light to shine within us, to give the light of revelation – the revelation of the glory of God in the face of Jesus Christ.

We are no better than pots of earthenware to contain this treasure, and this proves that such transcendent power does not come from us, but is God's alone. Hard-pressed on every side, we are never hemmed in; bewildered, we are never at our wits' end; hunted, we are never abandoned to our fate; struck down, we are not left to die. Wherever we go we carry death with us in our body, the death that Jesus died, that in this body also life may reveal itself, the life that Jesus lives.

Silent prayer of personal commitment and prayer for those charged with personal representative episcopal oversight within Christ's Church.

Feedback to the congregations
Create a humorous dialogue about 'heroes and hijackers' based on stereotypes about vicars and bishops, Methodist ministers and chapel stewards, etc. Display any key lessons learned as a result of the group work, and any steps forward that could be taken in your locality.

Action
Start planning how to work with people who continue to have anxieties and suspicions about any steps towards closer integration between Anglican and Methodist churches in response to God's mission.

Session six
Covenant
A psalm
Psalm 114: God keeps his promises
To ponder
How can we experience (and express) the difference between a covenant (centred on God) and a human contract?

A prayer of penitence
Almighty and everlasting God,
you hate nothing that you have made
and forgive the sins of all those who
   are penitent:
create and make in us new and
   contrite hearts
that we, worthily lamenting our sins
and acknowledging our
   wretchedness,
may receive from you, the God
   of all mercy,
perfect remission and forgiveness;
through Jesus Christ your Son
   our Lord,
who is alive and reigns with you,
in the unity of the Holy Spirit,
one God, now and for ever.

The Methodist Covenant Hymn
Come, let us use the grace divine,
And all, with one accord,
In a perpetual cov'nant join
Ourselves to Christ the Lord:

Give up ourselves, through Jesu's
   power,
His name to glorify;
And promise, in this sacred hour,
For God to live and die.

The cov'nant we this moment make
Be ever kept in mind:
We will no more our God forsake,
Or cast his words behind.

We never will throw off his fear
Who hears our solemn vow;
And if thou art well pleased to hear,
Come down, and meet us now.
To each the cov'nant blood apply,
Which takes our sins away;
And register our names on high,
And keep us to that day.

Informal prayer
For each other, for God's purposes in a broken world, for our own needs and for the needs of others.

Concluding prayer
Lord our God,
you have helped us by your grace
to make these prayers,
and you have promised through
   Christ our Lord
that when two or three agree in
   his name
you will grant what they ask.
Answer now your servants' prayers
according to their needs;
in this world grant that we may
   truly know you,
and in the world to come
graciously give us eternal life;
through Jesus Christ our Lord.
   Amen.

Feedback to the congregations
Make sure the text of the proposed national Covenant is available and introduce people to the seven affirmations and six commitments. Involve everyone in a time of prayer.

Action
Take the text of the Covenant together with suggestions for local initiatives to local denominational policy committees (e.g. Methodist circuit and church meetings, Parochial Church Councils, deanery synods etc.).

Set a timetable for meeting again to review what people have discussed and plan the next steps.

Make sure local Christian churches in other traditions are closely involved in the process. They will have much to give.

Material for worship during the optional workshop

A collect
O Lord God, just as you called Columba and Augustine, now you call us your servants to ventures of which we cannot see the ending, by paths as yet untrodden, through perils as yet unknown. Give us faith to go out with good courage, not knowing where we go, but only that your hand is leading us; through Jesus Christ our Lord.

Thanksgiving and self-offering

Leader: You found out what we were doing and you intervened.
'Come and do it together, Come and do it with me,' you said.

All: So, thank you, Lord, for intervening in our private lives.

Leader: You promised us nothing by way of success, recognition, possessions or reward. 'These things will come at the right time when you walk with me,' you said.

All: **So, thank you, Lord, for promising us nothing.**

Leader: You gave us no resources apart from ourselves – hands meant for caring, lips meant for praising, hearts meant for loving – and the Holy Spirit

to make us restless until we change.

All: **So, thank you, Lord, for the essential gifts.**

Leader: Then, just when we think we've got it right as to where we should go and what we should do; just when we're ready to take on the world, you come, like a beggar, to our back door, saying,
'This is the way. I am the Way'
and offering us bread and wine.

All: So, thank you, Lord, for coming again and keeping your word and showing you care for us and for all people.
Amen.

A concluding prayer
Eternal God, you have declared in Christ the completion of your purpose of love. May we live by faith, walk in hope, and be renewed by love, until the world reflects your glory and you are all in all.

Lord, when I am hungry give me someone to feed.
When I am thirsty give water for their thirst.

When I am sad, someone to lift from sorrow.
When burdens weigh upon me lay upon my shoulders the burden of my fellows.

When I stand greatly in need of tenderness, give me someone who yearns for love.

May your will be my bread;
your grace my strength;
your love my resting place.
Amen.

The Nicene Creed

It may prove useful to have this text available during Sessions four, six and during the workshop

We believe in one God,
the Father, the Almighty,
maker of heaven and earth,
of all that is, seen and unseen.

We believe in one Lord,
Jesus Christ,
the only Son of God,
eternally begotten of the Father,
God from God, Light from Light,
true God from true God,
begotten, not made,
of one Being with the Father;
through him all things were made.
For us and for our salvation
he came down from heaven,
was incarnate of the Holy Spirit
and the Virgin Mary
and became truly human.
For our sake he was crucified
under Pontius Pilate;
he suffered death and was buried.
On the third day he rose again
in accordance with the Scriptures;
he ascended into heaven
and is seated at the right hand
of the Father.
He will come again in glory to
judge the living and the dead,
and his kingdom will have no end.

We believe in the Holy Spirit,
the Lord, the giver of life,
who proceeds from the Father
and the Son,
who with the Father and the Son
is worshipped and glorified,
who has spoken through the
prophets.
We believe in one holy catholic
and apostolic Church.
We acknowledge one Baptism
for the forgiveness of sins.
We look for the resurrection
of the dead,
and the life of the world to come.
Amen.

Resources

The resources in this section are grouped under four headings:

1. Background reading and resources for the group sessions
2. Anglican and Methodist texts referred to in this study guide
3. Other ecumenical documents
4. Useful contacts.

Also included are the full texts of the Lambeth Quadrilateral (see p. 35) and the Nicene Creed (see p. 33).

1. Background reading and resources for the group sessions

Session one
- *Releasing Energy, How Methodists and Anglicans Can Work Together*, Church House Publishing and Methodist Publishing House, 2000.

- *Change Directions*, David Cormack, Monarch, 1995 (an illuminating book about coping with reality and coping with change).

Session two
- Look out for local history publications in your area describing church life in the nineteenth century.

- *Being Human Being Church*, Robert Warren, Marshall Pickering, 1995 (Robert Warren was formerly the Church of England's National Officer for Evangelism).

Session three
- 'The theological briefing pack' published with *An Anglican–Methodist Covenant, Common Statement of the Formal Conversations between the Methodist Church of Great Britain and the Church of England*, Methodist Publishing House and Church House Publishing, 2001. Available from the Council for Christian Unity.

- *Transforming Mission*, David Bosch, Orbis 1991 (for those who want a really authoritative presentation of mission theology – a big read!).

Session four
- *Baptism Eucharist and Ministry*, World Council of Churches, 1982.

- *Called to be One*, Churches Together in England, 1996.

Session five
- *Apostolicity and Succession*, Church House Publishing, 1994 (Church of England monograph on bishops).

- *Episcopé and Episcopacy*, in *Statements and Reports of the Methodist Church on Faith and Order 1993–2000*, volume 2, part 2, Methodist Publishing House, 2000 (Report to the Methodist Conference, 2000). Visit www.methodist.org.uk/information/episcopacy.htm

Session six
- *Covenant 21*, Baptist Union, 2001 (A renewal pack).

- *Changing World, Changing Church*, Michael Moynagh, Monarch, 2001 (A chance to look beyond the somewhat tedious business of trying to get two denominations to merge(!) and start considering some radical alternatives).

- *Changing Churches*, Jeanne Hinton, Churches Together in Britain and Ireland, 2002 (encouraging evidence of the gospel of love coming alive in everyday situations).

2. Some relevant Anglican and Methodist texts

- *An Anglican–Methodist Covenant, Common Statement of the Formal Conversations between the Methodist Church of Great Britain and the Church of England* (The Common Statement), Methodist Publishing House and Church House Publishing, 2001 (The Common Statement of the Anglican–Methodist Conversations which is the subject of this study guide).

- *Commitment to Mission and Unity: Report of the Informal Conversations between the Methodist Church and the Church of England*, Church House Publishing and Methodist Publishing House, 1996 (the discussions which led to the latest round of formal conversations).

- *Sharing in the Apostolic Communion*, Report of the Anglican–Methodist International Conversations, Anglican Communion Publications, 1996.

- *Called to Love and Praise: A Methodist Conference Statement on the Church*, Methodist Publishing House, 1999 (a mission agenda for local churches).

The Lambeth Quadrilateral

(See Session two p. 7 – and Session four p. 13)

This is to be found in two forms, from the Lambeth conferences of 1888 and 1920:

1888 Resolution 11

'That, in the opinion of this Conference, the following Articles supply a basis on which approach may be by God's blessing made towards Home Reunion:

(A) The Holy Scriptures of the Old and New Testaments, as 'containing all things necessary to salvation', and as being the rule and ultimate standard of faith.

(B) The Apostles' Creed, as the Baptismal Symbol; and the Nicene Creed, as the sufficient statement of the Christian faith.

(C) The two Sacraments ordained by Christ Himself – Baptism and the Supper of the Lord – ministered with unfailing use of Christ's words of Institution, and of the elements ordained by Him.

(D) The Historic Episcopate, locally adapted in the methods of its administration to the varying needs of the nations and people called of God into the Unity of His Church.'

As restated in 'An Appeal to All Christian People', adopted by resolution 9 of 1920

'VI. We believe that the visible unity of the Church will be found to involve the whole-hearted acceptance of:

The Holy Scriptures, as being the record of God's revelation of Himself to man, and as being the rule and ultimate standard of faith; and the Creed commonly called Nicene, as the sufficient statement of the Christian faith, and either it or the Apostles' Creed as the Baptismal confession of belief;

The divinely instituted sacraments of Baptism and the Holy Communion, as expressing for all the corporate life of the whole fellowship in and with Christ;

A ministry acknowledged by every part of the Church as possessing not only the inward call of the Spirit, but also the commission of Christ and the authority of the whole body.

VII. May we not reasonably claim that the Episcopate is the one means of providing such a ministry? . . .'

3. Other ecumenical documents

Conversations on the Way to Unity 1999–2001: The Report of the Informal Conversations between the Church of England, the Methodist Church and the United Reformed Church, United Reformed Church, 2001 (conversations which ran in parallel with the formal conversations that are the subject of this study guide).

Anglicans and Moravians: *Anglican–Moravian Conversations: The Fetter Lane Common Statement with Essays in Moravian and Anglican History*, Council for Christian Unity, 1996.

Anglican–Roman Catholic International Commission, *The Final Report*, CTS/SPCK, 1982.

Anglicans and French Reformed Churches: *Called to Witness and Service: The Reuilly Common Statement with Essays on Church, Eucharist and Ministry*, Church House Publishing, 1999.

Anglicans and German Evangelical Church (Lutheran): *The Meissen Agreement: Texts*, Council for Christian Unity, 1992.

British and Irish Anglicans and Nordic and Baltic Lutheran Churches: *The Porvoo Common Statement*, Church House Publishing, 1998.

4. Useful contacts
Denominations

Council for Christian Unity (Church of England) Church House, Great Smith Street, London SW1P 3NZ (020 7898 1479) www.cofe.anglican.org

Methodist Church House, 25 Marylebone Road, London NW1 5JR (020 7486 5502) www.methodist.org.uk

United Reformed Church, 86 Tavistock Place, London WC1H 9RT (020 7916 2020) www.urc.org.uk

The Baptist Union of Great Britain, Baptist House, PO Box 44, 129 Broadway, Didcot OX11 8RT (01235 517700) www.baptist.org.uk

Anglican Consultative Council, Anglican Communion Office, Partnership House, 157 Waterloo Road, London SE1 8UT www.anglicancommunion.org

Ecumenical bodies

Churches Together in England, 27 Tavistock Square, London WC1H 9HH (0207 529 8141) www.churches-together.org.uk

Churches Together in Britain and Ireland, Inter-Church House, 35–41 Lower Marsh, London SE1 7SA (020 7523 2121) www.ctbi.org.uk

Ecumenical officers

In almost every county, and in almost every Anglican diocese and Methodist district, specialist ecumenical officers are able to assist local churches.

If you cannot trace your local officers, contact Churches Together in England or the denominations who maintain up-to-date lists.

Feedback

Both the Church of England and the Methodist Church are eager to have feedback from local churches.

Alongside the formal processes of referral to denominational bodies such as diocesan and district synods, the two churches are keen to hear the experiences of groups who have used this study guide, and to gather stories of what local churches are deciding to do as a result.

Correspondence should be sent to the denominational offices listed above.

The Inherited Church

ANGELS? Naming why we feel we can't go on as we are	DEMONS? Naming the good things we fear to put at risk

The Emerging Church

ANGELS? Naming our calling to be committed to the needs of people around us	DEMONS? Naming our fears for the future and the constraints from the present

Belief

The things I believe very strongly

The things I have difficulty believing

Experience

The times when God has seemed very close

The times when God has seemed very remote – and it has been hard to stay faithful

Koinonia
Communicatio

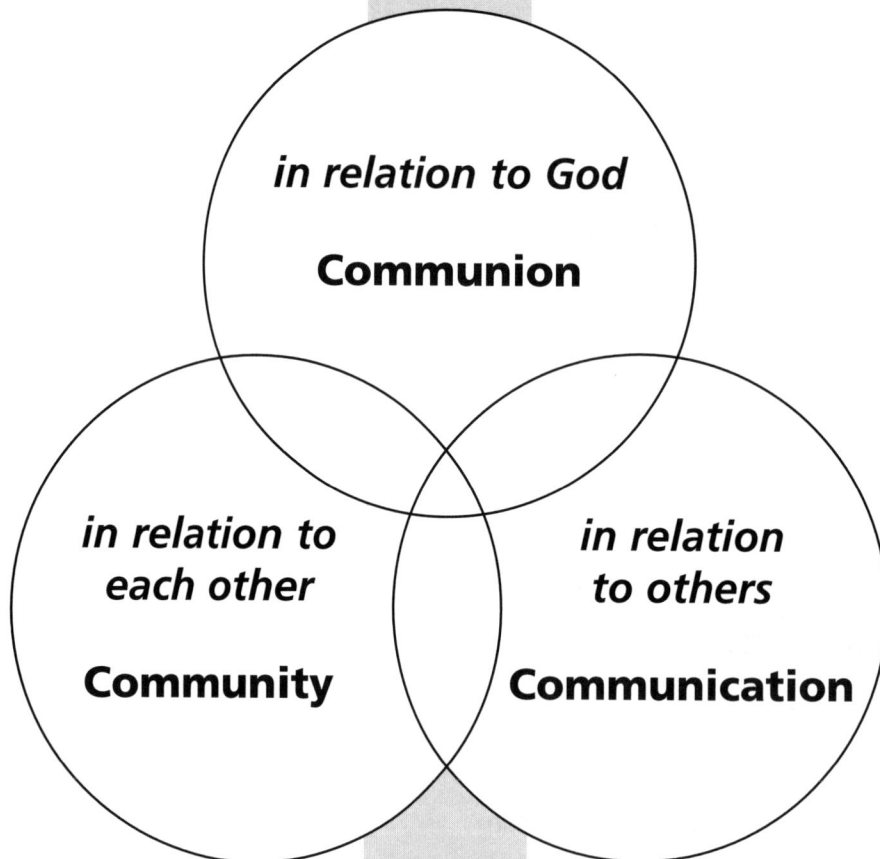

in relation to God

Communion

*in relation to
each other*

Community

*in relation
to others*

Communication

The Work of
The Holy Spirit

As you view the displays and read the feedback, compare the churches.

On the time charts,
look out for:

Different ways the stories are told:
Do they tell the story of the church
or of the community?
The effect of what happened on church life.
When churches co-operated (or didn't).
Anything unusual.

On the local maps,
look out for:

Areas where there are no churchgoers.
Where church members come from
(differences between the churches).
The 'disadvantaged' parts of your area.

Make notes on this sheet under these headings:

1. Pleasant surprises	2. Things that concern or disturb you	3. Needs or opportunities that occur to you

Acknowledgements

The publisher gratefully acknowledges permission to reproduce copyright material in this book. Every effort has been made to trace and contact copyright holders. If there are any inadvertent omissions we apologize to those concerned and undertake to include suitable acknowledgements in any future edition.

The General Synod of the Anglican Church of Canada: 'God of compassion' (**29**) from *The Book of Alternative Services of the Anglican Church of Canada*, copyright © 1985

The Archbishops' Council: *Commitment to Mission and Unity*, Church House Publishing and The Methodist Publishing House, 1996 (**9**); 'Lord our God, in our sin' (**29**), 'O King enthroned on high' (**30**), 'Jesus Christ, risen Master and triumphant Lord' (**31**), 'Almighty and everlasting God' (**32**) from *Common Worship: Services and Prayers for the Church of England*, Church House Publishing, 2000; 'Now that we have been put right with God' (**31**) from *Patterns for Worship*, Church House Publishing, 1995.

The Archbishops' Council and the Trustees for Methodist Church Purposes: *An Anglican–Methodist Covenant: Common Statement of the Formal Conversations between the Methodist Church of Great Britain and the Church of England*, Methodist Publishing House and Church House Publishing, 2001 (**vii, 2, 3, 6, 7, 8, 9, 10, 11, 14, 15, 17, 18, 19, 23, 27, 35**)

Cambridge University Press: Extract from 2 Corinthians 4. 5-10 (**32**) from *New English Bible* © Oxford University Press and Cambridge University Press 1961, 1970.

Churches Together in Britain and Ireland: 'Lord, when I am hungry' (**33**), *All Year Round*, British Council of Churches, 1989

Glenstal Common Eucharist: 'O Lord God, just as you called Columba and Augustine' (**33**), 1985, unpublished

Revd Dr Ivor H. Jones: 'Christ, our King before creation' (**30**); F. Pratt Green: 'Christ is the world's light' (**31**); *Hymns and Psalms*, Methodist Publishing House, 1983

Kingsway's Thankyou Music: 'From heav'n you came, helpless babe' (**30**), adm. by worshiptogether.com songs excl. UK and Europe, adm. by Kingsway Music, tyn@kingsway.co.uk Used by permission.

Trustees for Methodist Church Purposes: *Sharing in the Apostolic Communion*, Anglo-Methodist International Commission, 1996 (**9**); *Called to Love and Praise: A Methodist Conference Statement on the Church*, Methodist Publishing House, 1999 (**9**); 'Have mercy on me, O God' (**29**), 'In faith we pray to God' (**30**), 'Gracious God, your Son Jesus Christ' (**30**), 'Gracious and holy God' (**31**), 'Come, let us use the grace divine' (**32**), 'Lord our God, you have helped us' (**32**), *The Methodist Worship Book*, Methodist Publishing House, 1999 ; *The Methodist Conference Resolution 2000* (**18**), copyright © The Conference Office, 25 Marylebone Road, London NW1 5JR

Wild Goose Publications: 'Will you come and follow me' (**29**) from *Heaven Shall not Wait*, words John L. Bell and Graham Maule, music 'Kelvingrove' Scottish trad., words and arrangement © 1987 WGRG; 'You found out what we were doing' (**33**), *The Wee Worship Book*, © 1999 WGRG, Iona Community, Glasgow G2 3DH. Reprinted with permission.

L. M. Willis: 'Father, hear the prayer we offer' (**31**), *Hymns Ancient and Modern New Standard*, Hymns Ancient and Modern Ltd, 1983